REGENTS RENAISSANCE DRAMA SERIES

General Editor : Cyrus Hoy
Advisory Editor : G. E. Bentley

THE BROKEN HEART

JOHN FORD

The Broken Heart

Edited by

DONALD K. ANDERSON, JR.

A BISON BOOK

UNIVERSITY OF NEBRASKA PRESS · LINCOLN

Regents Renaissance Drama Series

The purpose of the Regents Renaissance Drama Series is to provide soundly edited texts, in modern spelling, of the more significant plays of the Elizabethan, Jacobean, and Caroline theater. Each text in the series is based on a fresh collation of all sixteenth- and seventeenth-century editions. The textual notes, which appear above the line at the bottom of each page, record all substantive departures from the edition used as the copy-text. Variant substantive readings among sixteenth- and seventeenth-century editions are listed there as well. In cases where two or more of the old editions present widely divergent readings, a list of substantive variants in editions through the seventeenth century is given in an appendix. Editions after 1700 are referred to in the textual notes only when an emendation originating in some one of them is received into the text. Variants of accidentals (spelling, punctuation, capitalization) are not recorded in the notes. Contracted forms of characters' names are silently expanded in speech prefixes and stage directions, and, in the case of speech prefixes, are regularized. Additions to the stage directions of the copy-text are enclosed in brackets. Stage directions such as "within" or "aside" are enclosed in parentheses when they occur in the copy-text.

Spelling has been modernized along consciously conservative lines. "Murther" has become "murder," and "burthen," "burden," but within the limits of a modernized text, and with the following exceptions, the linguistic quality of the original has been carefully preserved. The variety of contracted forms ('em, 'am, 'm, 'um, 'hem) used in the drama of the period for the pronoun *them* are here regularly given as 'em, and the alternation between a'th' and o'th' (for *on* or *of the*) is regularly reproduced as o'th'. The copy-text distinction between preterite endings in -d and -ed is preserved except where the elision of *e* occurs in the penultimate syllable; in such cases, the final syllable is contracted. Thus, where the old editions read "threat'ned," those of the present series read "threaten'd." Where, in the old editions, a contracted preterite in -y'd would yield -i'd in modern spelling (as in "try'd," "cry'd," "deny'd"), the word is here given in its full form (e.g., "tried," "cried," "denied").

Punctuation has been brought into accord with modern practices. The effort here has been to achieve a balance between the generally light pointing of the old editions, and a system of punctuation which, without overloading the text with exclamation marks, semicolons, and dashes, will make the often loosely flowing verse (and prose) of the original syntactically intelligible to the modern reader. Dashes are regularly used only to indicate interrupted speeches, or shifts of address within a single speech.

Explanatory notes, chiefly concerned with glossing obsolete words and phrases, are printed below the textual notes at the bottom of each page. References to stage directions in the notes follow the admirable system of the Revels editions, whereby stage directions are keyed, decimally, to the line of the text before or after which they occur. Thus, a note on 0.2 has reference to the second line of the stage direction at the beginning of the scene in question. A note on 115.1 has reference to the first line of the stage direction following line 115 of the text of the relevant scene.

CYRUS HOY

University of Rochester

Contents

List of Abbreviations

corr.	corrected
DNB	*Dictionary of National Biography*
Halliwell	James O. Halliwell. *A Dictionary of Archaic and Provincial Words.* 11th ed. 2 vols. London, 1889.
L and S	Henry G. Liddell and Robert Scott. *A Greek-English Lexicon.* 9th ed. Oxford, 1951.
Lawrence	William J. Lawrence. *Pre-Restoration Stage Studies.* Cambridge, Mass., 1927.
Nares	Robert Nares. *A Glossary; or, Collection of Words, Phrases, Names, and Allusions to Customs, Proverbs, &c. which have been thought to require Illustration, in the Works of English Authors, particularly Shakespeare, and his Contemporaries.* 2 vols. London, 1822.
OED	*Oxford English Dictionary*
Pliny	*Natural History.* Trans. H. Rackham (Loeb Classical Library). London, 1938. (Gaius Plinius Secundus completed *Naturalis Historia* in 77 A.D.)
S.D.	stage direction
S.P.	speech prefix
Tilley	Morris P. Tilley. *A Dictionary of the Proverbs in England in the Sixteenth and Seventeenth Centuries.* Ann Arbor, 1950.
uncorr.	uncorrected

EDITIONS

Q	*The Broken Heart. A Tragedy.* London, 1633.
Weber	Henry Weber, ed. *The Dramatic Works of John Ford.* Edinburgh, 1811. Vol. I.
Gifford	William Gifford, ed. *The Dramatic Works of John Ford.* London, 1827. Vol. I.

Coleridge — Hartley Coleridge, ed. *The Dramatic Works of Massinger and Ford*. London, 1840.

Dyce — Rev. Alexander Dyce, ed. (additions to and revisions of Gifford). *The Works of John Ford*. London, 1869. Vol. I.

Ellis — Havelock Ellis, ed. *John Ford* (Mermaid Series). London, 1888.

Scollard — Clinton Scollard, ed. *The Broken Heart*. New York, 1895.

Sherman — S. P. Sherman, ed. *Ford's 'Tis Pity and The Broken Heart* (Belles-Lettres Series). Boston, 1915.

Oliphant — E. H. C. Oliphant, ed. *Shakespeare and His Fellow Dramatists*. New York, 1929.

Spencer — Hazelton Spencer, ed. *Elizabethan Plays*. Boston, 1933.

BHN — Charles R. Baskervill, Virgil B. Heltzel, and Arthur H. Nethercot, eds. *Elizabethan and Stuart Plays*. New York, 1934.

Harrier — Richard C. Harrier, ed. *An Anthology of Jacobean Drama*. New York, 1963. Vol. II.

Morris — Brian Morris, ed. *The Broken Heart* (The New Mermaids). London, 1965.

Introduction

With its theme of thwarted love and its tone of stoical restraint, *The Broken Heart. A Tragedy*, first published in 1633, has generally been considered one of the best, if not the best, of John Ford's plays. Among the many nineteenth- and twentieth-century critics admiring it are Charles Lamb (1808), Algernon Charles Swinburne (1875), and T. S. Eliot (1932).[1] Its principal story, for which there is no known literary source, can be told briefly. Orgilus and Penthea, in love, are betrothed; but Penthea's brother, Ithocles, insists that she wed Bassanes, an older man. The marriage is a miserable one, Bassanes being a doting and insanely jealous husband and Penthea a dutiful but grief-stricken wife. Meanwhile, Ithocles falls in love with Calantha, the princess of Sparta, who accepts him as her suitor and obtains the consent of her father, King Amyclas, to marry him. But Penthea, who has lost the will to live, dies; consequently, Orgilus, holding Ithocles responsible for his sister's tragedy, murders him. Calantha—now a queen, her father having died—sentences Orgilus to death, arranges for the disposition of her kingdom, puts a wedding ring on the finger of the slain Ithocles (her "contracted lord" and "neglected husband"), and dies of a broken heart.

In his play, Ford emphasizes that marriage must be based upon love. To be sure, a woman must have the consent of her father (or brother), but, even more important, the latter must not enforce marriage when it is not desired. Ithocles is an obvious offender in this respect, and his tyrannical treatment of his sister ultimately destroys them both. Other characters—Orgilus, King Amyclas of Sparta, and Prince Nearchus of Argos—avoid the error of Ithocles. Early in the play it seems that Orgilus will oppose the marriage of his sister, Euphranea, to Prophilus, closest friend of Ithocles, but he later

[1] Lamb, *Specimens of the English Dramatic Poets* (London, 1897), p. 228; Swinburne, "John Ford" in *Complete Works*, ed. Sir Edmund Gosse and Thomas J. Wise (London, 1926), XII, 380–381; and Eliot, *Selected Essays 1917–1932* (London, 1932), pp. 198–200.

sanctions it; and the bridal song at the wedding of these lovers describes the marital happiness that is to be theirs:

> *Comforts lasting, loves increasing,*
> *Like soft hours never ceasing;* ...
> *Hearts by holy union wedded*
> *More than theirs by custom bedded* ...
> (III.iv.70–71, 74–75)

King Amyclas, father of Calantha, though welcoming Prince Nearchus as her suitor, states his desire "Not to enforce affection by our will,/ But by her own choice to confirm it gladly" (III.iii.11–12). Nearchus agrees, and when subsequently learning that Calantha and Ithocles are in love, decides to promote their marriage; his reason he confides to a friend, Amelus: "affections injur'd/ By tyranny or rigor of compulsion,/ .... Ne'er spring to timely growth. Observe, for instance,/ Life-spent Penthea and unhappy Orgilus" (IV.ii.205–206, 208–209). Hence Calantha and Ithocles are free to marry, though their joy is to be shattered by the avenging dagger of Orgilus.

The central figure of the drama is Penthea. She sets the dominant tone of heartbreak and hopelessness; hers are the most moving speeches. Between her first appearance (II.i) and her death (IV.iii), she is the principal figure in four scenes. Three of them are private, intensely personal conversations with Orgilus (II.iii), Ithocles (III.ii), and Calantha (III.v); in the fourth scene (IV.ii), a climactic one, she has lost her mind, and speaks with great pathos to Orgilus, Bassanes, and Ithocles, as in the following lines:

> Sure if we were all sirens we should sing pitifully,
> And 'twere a comely music when in parts
> One sung another's knell. The turtle sighs
> When he hath lost his mate, and yet some say
> 'A must be dead first. 'Tis a fine deceit
> To pass away in a dream. Indeed I've slept
> With mine eyes open a great while. No falsehood
> Equals a broken faith. There's not a hair
> Sticks on my head but like a leaden plummet
> It sinks me to the grave. I must creep thither;
> The journey is not long. (IV.ii.69–79)

Her end is marked by a "deathful air" sung off-stage ("Now love dies, implying/ Love's martyrs must be ever, ever dying"), then "a horrid stillness" (IV.iii.151–154). Chiefly from Penthea emanates the preternatural calm, even immobility, of the drama. Indeed, she dies in a chair, where she has been awaiting death; so does her brother, a few minutes later, in a chair next to hers. Also contributing to this general effect is the striking and at times almost exaggerated composure of other characters: Bassanes, upon learning of his wife's madness; Orgilus, when bleeding himself to death; and Calantha, who continues to dance while being informed of the deaths of King Amyclas, Penthea, and Ithocles and who, noting "the silent griefs which cut the heartstrings" (V.iii.75), dies smiling.

Ford's handling of plot, particularly the revenge of Orgilus, deserves attention. Although the initial cause of Orgilus' bitterness (Ithocles' breaking of his betrothal to Penthea) has already occurred when the play begins, not until Penthea has lost her mind (IV.ii), indicated her own imminent death, and pointed an accusing finger at her brother, does he decide to murder Ithocles. Earlier Orgilus' attitudes are ominous but hardly homicidal: he seemingly will resist the match between Euphranea and Prophilus, but eventually yields to various pressures, principally the desires of the king and of his father; disguised as a scholar, he meets Penthea in the palace grove and claims her as his own, but accedes to her demand that he never again speak to her of love; abandoning his disguise, returning to court, and being sought as friend by Ithocles (III.iii), he often replies to the latter with terse and sinister irony, but even as late as the end of the first scene of Act IV his soliloquy reveals not only blindness to the implications of Tecnicus' prophecy—"*Let craft with courtesy a while confer,/ Revenge proves its own executioner*"—but lack of murderous intent. Thus in the first three and one half acts the revenge motif, while present, is not dominant; both Penthea's breakdown and the love affair between Ithocles and Calantha receive greater emphasis. Yet Ford's timing is such that Orgilus' vengeance, when it does occur, is doubly effective, because now Ithocles is himself betrothed and therefore atones fully for his sister's loss of love and life.

Scholars of Ford have pointed to possible influences, both specific and general, on *The Broken Heart*. William Hazlitt (1820) believes that the interrupted dance (V.ii) was suggested by a scene (V.vi) in John Marston's *The Malcontent* (1604);[2] William Gifford (1827) notes a similarity between Orgilus' use of a mechanical chair in murdering

[2] Hazlitt, *Lectures on the Dramatic Literature of the Age of Elizabeth* in *Complete Works*, ed. P. P. Howe (London, 1931), VI, 270–272.

Ithocles (IV.iv) and a scene (I.v) in Barnabe Barnes' *The Devil's Charter* (1606);[3] C. R. Baskervill (1913) thinks that Ford may be indebted to a novella by the Italian Bandello for the conversation between Orgilus and Crotolon (I.i) concerning the marriage of Euphranea;[4] and Robert Davril (1954) sees as a likely source, for Calantha's wedding the crowned corpse of Ithocles (V.iii), *Doña Inès de Castro*, a tragedy by the Spanish playwright La Cerda, and he also cites, as an earlier portrayal of Ford's general theme, George Wilkins' play *The Miseries of Enforced Marriage* (1607).[5] Here one should add, as a possible origin for Orgilus' bleeding to death (V.ii), a scene (V.i) in William D'Avenant's *The Cruel Brother* (1630), in which Corsa so dies, her brother Foreste cutting her wrist-veins.[6]

Stuart Sherman (1909) believes the play is based upon the relationship of Sir Philip Sidney and Penelope Devereux, seeing a significant likeness between the ill-starred love of Orgilus and Penthea and the enforced marriage of Penelope to Lord Rich despite her being promised to Sidney.[7] Ford's knowledge of this matter is indicated by his earlier poem *Fame's Memorial* (1606), which is dedicated to Penelope and is an elegy on the death of her second husband, the Earl of Devonshire, whom she married after divorcing Lord Rich. More recent commentators vary in their estimates of Sherman's hypothesis, some minimizing and others substantially accepting it. S. Blaine Ewing (1940) contends, with considerable documentation, that Ford's characterization of Bassanes owes much to Robert Burton's *The Anatomy of Melancholy* (1621), that the symptoms of the elderly husband's jealousy (II.i)—his groundless fears of adultery, his sudden furies towards his servant Phulas, his sweating, his headache—come from those sections of *The Anatomy* devoted to jealousy and to love melancholy.[8] George Sensabaugh (1944) believes that Ford's treatment of love is influenced by the Platonic coterie at the court of

[3] Gifford, ed., *The Dramatic Works of John Ford* (London, 1827), I, 302–303.

[4] Baskervill, "Bandello and *The Broken Heart*," *Modern Language Notes*, XXVIII (1913), 51–52.

[5] Davril, *Le Drame de John Ford* (Paris, 1954), pp. 176–178.

[6] *Works*, ed. James Maidment and W. H. Logan (Edinburgh, 1872), I, 182–183.

[7] Sherman, "Stella and *The Broken Heart*," *Publications of the Modern Language Association of America*, XXIV (1909), 274–285.

[8] Ewing, *Burtonian Melancholy in the Plays of John Ford* (Princeton, 1940), pp. 17–21, 56–60.

Queen Henrietta Maria, wife of Charles I.[9] Davril disagrees, claiming that the coterie flourished after Ford had written most or all of his plays and pointing out that as early as 1606 Ford himself, in his pamphlet *Honor Triumphant*, had shown much interest in Platonic and chivalric ideals.[10]

Whether one shares Sensabaugh's opinion or Davril's, *The Broken Heart* undeniably idealizes both beauty and love. Beauty is emphasized in the listing of the dramatis personae, whose names are "fitted to their qualities": Calantha is "Flower of Beauty" and Ithocles "Honor of Loveliness." Both Calantha and Penthea are beautiful women, and throughout the play the beauty they manifest is worshipped. Ithocles, when reproached by Prince Nearchus for rudeness to him in courting Calantha, replies: "There is more divinity/ In beauty than in majesty" (IV.i.95–96); and earlier Nearchus, speaking to Calantha, declares himself a subject "to beauty's scepter./ As all hearts kneel, so mine" (III.iii.42–43). Penthea's beauty is similarly adored by Orgilus and Bassanes. But the clearest instance of Ford's Platonism occurs in the first of the play's four songs; after a catalogue of impossibilities, couched in the form of questions (*"Can you paint a thought . . . Can you grasp a sigh or . . . Rob a virgin's honor chastely?"*) comes the answer:

> *Yet you may*
> *Sooner do both that and this . . .*
> *Than by any praise display*
> *Beauty's beauty; such a glory*
> *As beyond all fate, all story.*
> (III.ii.7–8, 10–12)

Also Platonic is Ford's treatment of love, stressing as it does the eternal union of two souls. Orgilus, referring to Penthea and himself, tells his father Crotolon that "an interchange/ Of holy and chaste love, so fix'd our souls/ In a firm growth of union, that no time/ Can eat into the pledge" (I.i.29–32), and he later (II.iii.40–41) describes their love as "that precious figure/ Seal'd with the lively stamp of equal souls." The bridal song at the wedding of Euphranea and Prophilus—"*Hearts by holy union wedded/ More than theirs by custom*

[9] Sensabaugh, *The Tragic Muse of John Ford* (Stanford, 1944), the chapter entitled "Unbridled Individualism," pp. 94–173.

[10] Davril, pp. 351–352.

bedded"—makes the same point. In at least one important respect, however, Ford's concept of love differs from that of those court, or coterie, Platonics who maintained that spiritual union was sufficient. Both Orgilus—"the body pines,/ Not relishing the real taste of food" (II.iii.36–37)—and Ithocles—"Give me felicity/ Of which my senses waking are partakers,/ A real, visible, material happiness" (IV.i.48–50)—desire physical consummation, and Penthea laments the "Divorce betwixt my body and my heart" (II.iii.57). Both men liken love to banquets that are to be eaten; Penthea starves to death for want of love as well as food.

Clifford Leech (1957) finds in Ford's plays what he calls an "aristocratic ideal": "His most impressive characters have an aristocratic code of endurance, remembering always in their anguish that they are courtiers and princes." [11] He cites, as his first example, Calantha's final actions and words, and finds a similar poise in Penthea, Ithocles, and Orgilus. [12] There is such a code in *The Broken Heart*, perhaps one even more extensive than Leech has described. For the standards of courtesy and propriety in Ford's Sparta are high, and so frequently are they applied that one is tempted to label the drama a "tragedy of manners." The two extremes in this respect are the frenzied intrusion of Bassanes, poniard in hand, upon the conversation between Penthea and Ithocles (III.ii)—which prompts Ithocles to remark "The meaning of this rudeness?" and "I'd say you were unmannerly"—and the regal decorum of Calantha when, a dance having been thrice interrupted by those reporting the deaths of Amyclas, Penthea, and Ithocles, she says, "'tis, methinks, a rare presumption/ In any who prefers our lawful pleasures/ Before their own sour censure, to interrupt/ The custom of this ceremony bluntly" (V.ii.24–27). In Ford's play, the higher one's rank, the more polished his manners: Princess Calantha and Prince Nearchus are flawless; Ithocles, Orgilus, and Penthea are at times censurers and at other times the censured; Prophilus is socially remiss at least twice; and the courtiers Hemophil and Groneas are utterly gauche. Ithocles on three occasions is reprimanded by Nearchus, who regards him as an uncouth soldier: "A gallant man at arms is here, a doctor/ In feats of chivalry, blunt and rough-spoken,/ Vouchsafing not the fustian of civility,/ Which less rash spirits style good manners" (IV.i.85–88).

[11] Leech, *John Ford and the Drama of His Time* (London, 1957), p. 12.
[12] *Ibid.*, pp. 12–13, 86–91.

One also should note the unusual pattern of the play's verbal structure, which reveals the author's poetic sensitivity. The language abounds with echoes and connections, many of them doubtless conscious and deliberate—those in the four lyrics, for example—but many of them probably not, indicating a feeling for words much deeper than the surface of the mind; in this respect Ford would seem to excel his Caroline contemporaries Massinger and Shirley. His portrayal of Ithocles is an instance. Time and again Ithocles is described in terms of rising and falling, the former usually presumptuous and the latter usually precipitous. Thus, soliloquizing on his ambition, he likens it to a seeled dove that mounts to clouds only to tumble "headlong down" (II.ii.3–5) and to fireworks that "fly into the air" only to "vanish/ In stench and smoke" (II.ii.6–8). Armostes compares him to Ixion, who, "aiming/ To embrace Juno, bosom'd but a cloud/ And begat centaurs" (IV.i.69–71); Orgilus compares him to Phaeton (IV.iv.26), who drove the sun-chariot until blasted from the heavens by Zeus; and Bassanes likens him to both Ixion and Phaeton (III.ii.130–131). Prince Nearchus cites his "colossic greatness" (IV.i.94), warns him that "low mushrooms never rival cedars" (IV.i.98), and refers to him as "lord ascendant" (IV.ii.200), while Orgilus, in an aside, says, "The youth is up on tiptoe, yet may stumble" (IV.iii.92). The cumulative effect of these descriptions is to make Ithocles an upstart and to prefigure his sudden downfall.

Analysis finds another interesting verbal pattern for Bassanes' jealousy. Here metaphor and tone are dominated by the bestial, which depicts Bassanes' attitudes towards others and, eventually, towards himself, and which also describes at times the attitudes of others towards him. The bestial early appears in Bassanes' fear-laden commands and threats (II.i) as he calls his servants Phulas and Grausis "son of a cat," "ill-looking hound's-head," "magpie," and "damnable bitch-fox," epithets sometimes uttered in asides that interrupt his adulation of his wife and hence become a sort of counterpoint; the bestial is utilized by Phulas when, sensing his master's overpowering jealousy, he describes to Bassanes five unexpected guests as "a herd of lords," "a flock of ladies," "shoals of horses," and "caroches in drifts" (II.i.128–130). Later in the play Bassanes uses animal imagery on two important occasions: when he accuses Ithocles of incest—"one that franks his lust/ In swine-security of bestial incest" (III.ii.149–150)—and when he realizes how terribly he has wronged Penthea—"And of those beasts/ The worst am I"

(IV.ii.28–29). One feels this continuity of tone and metaphor to be, on the part of Ford, more instinctive than contrived. His use of the word *monster* suggests the same kind of verbal unifying: in Act I, Orgilus describes Bassanes' jealousy as "a kind of monster-love" (I.i.61); in Act II, Bassanes injects into his account of "the joys of marriage" an aside as to the whereabouts of Grausis, "a new monster" (II.ii.92); and in Act III, Ithocles, having been accused by Bassanes of incest, calls him "Monster!" (III.ii.153).

As for Penthea, her wronged innocence is imaged in several ways. Three times she is associated with the turtle-dove (III.ii.87, IV.ii.71–73, and IV.iv.29), and three times she is likened to a shrine or temple (I.i.64, III.ii.85, and IV.ii.32); as the wife of Bassanes, however, she conceives of herself, in act though not in desire, as a wanton: a "faith-breaker" (III.ii.69), "spotted whore" (III.ii.70), and one whose "name is strumpeted" (IV.ii.148). Sometimes Ford seems to initiate in Penthea a verbal linkage with other characters or parts of the play. For example, her preference, expressed to Bassanes, for "the inward fashion" of her mind to the "gaudy outsides" of fine clothes (II.i.98–99) is echoed not only in her husband's futile attempt to cure her neurosis—"there is a mastery/ In art to fatten and keep smooth the outside" (IV.ii.162–163)—but also in the song Princess Calantha has prepared for her own death: "*Glories, pleasures, pomps, delights, and ease/ Can but please/ Th'outward senses when the mind/ Is not untroubled or by peace refin'd*" (V.iii.81–84). Indeed, one wonders, concerning the deaths of Penthea and Calantha, if the two events are not connected as much by the pattern of Ford's language as by the sequence of his plot. There is, for instance, considerable similarity between the dirge for Calantha (V.iii.81–94) and Penthea's earlier lament to her (III.v.13–23); also, though Penthea unquestionably is mad when she says "Sure if we were all sirens we should sing pitifully,/ And 'twere a comely music when in parts/ One sung another's knell" (IV.ii.69–71), the reader should bear in mind that knells are to be sung for both women (IV.iii and V.iii), Calantha's in parts and by three voices.

But there is more to Ford's dramaturgy than words. *The Broken Heart* was written to be seen as well as heard, and the visual aspects of the play—whether considered as simply gesture and posture, or as spectacle and emblem—contribute greatly to its unique effectiveness. Usually their arrangement seems more intentional than Ford's verbal patterns and at times verges on artificiality, yet the ultimate result is to enhance, not impair, the dignity and restraint of his personae; if they are self-conscious, even ceremonious, they are so not about trivia but about love and death. Calantha's decorous and deliberate response to the three messages of death (V.ii) may seem like part of a masque or ballet, but the playwright, after all, is endeavoring to portray stoicism, not spontaneity. *The Broken Heart*, furthermore, contains much repetition of the visual. The love of Penthea and Orgilus is thus portrayed. When they meet in the grove, Penthea clasps his hand, kisses it, and kneels before him; then he too kneels (II.iii.64–67). Later (IV.ii.110–126) Penthea, in her madness, once more clasps his hand and kisses it; then he kisses hers. To depict the relationship between Penthea and Ithocles, Ford again uses repetition, but this time of posture rather than gesture; sister and brother are sedentary, in chairs close together, both in their long conversation (III.ii) and in death (IV.iv). Visual parallels connect the deaths of Ithocles (IV.iv) and Orgilus (V.ii): both men bleed to death, are stabbed more than once (and by the same dagger), assume an unflinching attitude, and are helped to bleed more rapidly by an efficient and admiring attendant. The play's most spectacular scene is the final one; ceremonial throughout, it begins as coronation and worship, changes to testament, and culminates as marriage and funeral. Vivid in itself, it acquires additional luster from pictorial associations with earlier scenes, such as Calantha's crowning Ithocles with a garland (I.ii) and casting her ring at his feet (IV.i), and Penthea's bequeathing Ithocles to Calantha (III.v) and joining him in a tableau of death (IV.iv). Ford's handling of sight and sound accounts in no small way for the peculiar appeal and excellence of *The Broken Heart*.

THE DATE AND THE TEXT

On March 28, 1633, *The Broken Heart* was entered in the Stationers' Register by its publisher, Hugh Beeston:

Hugh Beeston   Entred for his Copy vnder the hands of Sir HENRY HERBERT and/ master Aspley Warden a Tragedy called *The broken heart* by JOHN/ FFORD.[13]

---

[13] *A Transcript of the Registers of the Company of Stationers in London; 1554–1640 A.D.*, ed. Edward Arber (London, 1875–1894), IV, 294.

The play was printed in the same year (the only seventeenth-century edition), with the following title page for the quarto:

THE/ BROKEN HEART./ A Tragedy./ ACTED/ By the KINGS Majesties Seruants/ at the priuate House in the/ BLACK-FRIERS./ *Fide Honor*./ [ornament]/ LONDON./ Printed by I. B. for HVGH BEESTON, and are to/ be sold at his Shop, neere the *Castle* in/ *Corne-hill*, 1633.

When Ford wrote *The Broken Heart* is not known. Gerald Bentley suggests 1627–1631 as a likely period for its composition:

Twelve of Ford's seventeen known plays can be assigned to acting companies on the basis of external evidence. Eliminating the collaborations with Dekker, we find that three plays were performed by the King's company and five by [Christopher] Beeston's companies at the Phoenix. None of the plays for Beeston can be shown to be before 1630, but of the three for the King's company *The Lover's Melancholy* was licensed by Herbert 24 November 1628, *Beauty in a Trance* [lost] was acted at court 28 November 1630, and the third is *The Broken Heart*. It seems to me that the few facts we have suggest that, after he ceased to collaborate with Dekker, Ford wrote three or more plays for the King's company; then, at least a year or so before 1633 (since the Queen's play, *Love's Sacrifice*, was licensed 21 January 1632/33, and both it and *'Tis Pity* were published as Queen's plays in 1633), he made some sort of agreement with Christopher Beeston and wrote all the rest of his plays for the management of the Phoenix. If this is the case, *The Broken Heart* must have been close in date to *Beauty in a Trance* and *The Lover's Melancholy*, or about 1627–31.[14]

Ford's authorship is proven not only by the inclusion of his name in the Stationers' Register entry (see above) but also, in the quarto itself, by his name (*Iohn Ford*) following the dedicatory epistle to Lord Craven and by the appearance on the title page of his anagram, *Fide Honor* (i.e., "Iohn Forde"), which is found in several of his other plays.

The printer "I. B." listed on the title page is undoubtedly John Beale, for two ornaments in the quarto are identical to ones found in

[14] Gerald E. Bentley, *The Jacobean and Caroline Stage* (Oxford, 1941–1956), III, 441–442.

works printed by "I. Beale" in 1633. One is the ornamental initial "T" that begins Ford's dedication on sig. A2^r;[15] it also appears on sig. B1^r of John Preston's *Sins overthrow* (*Short Title Catalogue*, #20275). The other is the floral headpiece at the beginning of Ford's Act I on sig. B1^r; it appears both in the second edition of Preston's book (*STC*, #20276) at the top of sig. A1^r and twice in Nathanael Cole's *The Godly Mans Assurance* (*STC*, #5537), on pages 296 (V3^v) and 324 (Y1^v). Beale was from 1612 to 1641 the head of a printing house on Fetter Lane; among the better-known works coming from his press are Bacon's *Essays* (both the 1612 and 1639 editions) and Jonson's *Bartholomew Fair* (1631).[16]

Hugh Beeston, the bookseller listed on the title page, published three of Ford's plays: *The Broken Heart* and *Love's Sacrifice* in 1633 and *Perkin Warbeck* in 1634.[17] As the imprint on the title page (which page was, in effect, an advertisement) tells us, Beeston's bookshop was "neere the *Castle* in *Corne-hill*." Cornhill was an east-west street that ran past the Royal Exchange; on the north side of this street, near the Exchange, was the Castle Tavern.[18]

"The KINGS Majesties Seruants," or the King's company (of which Shakespeare had been a member), was the most active theatrical company at this time, performing during the summers at the Globe and for the rest of the year at its "priuate House in the BLACK-FRIERS," the former monastery.[19]

The present edition is based upon a collation of seven copies of the quarto: the Folger and Library of Congress copies in the original, and the Yale, British Museum (B.M.12.g.3[6]), Harvard, University of Texas, and Boston Public Library copies in Xerox prints. Alterations were made in the text while sheets were passing through Beale's press. Corrections, in substantives and accidentals, have been found

[15] According to W. W. Greg, this leaf should have been signed "A3," the "A2" signature being a misprint. See Greg, *A Bibliography of the English Printed Drama to the Restoration* (London, 1939–1959), II, 627 (#480).

[16] Henry R. Plomer, *A Dictionary of the Booksellers and Printers Who Were at Work in England, Scotland, and Ireland from 1641–1667* (London, 1907), pp. 17–18.

[17] R. B. McKerrow, *A Dictionary of Printers and Booksellers in England, Scotland, and Ireland, and of Foreign Printers of English Books, 1557–1640* (London, 1910), p. 29.

[18] E./H. Sugden, *A Topographical Dictionary to the Works of Shakespeare and His Fellow Dramatists* (Manchester, 1925), pp. 105 and 131.

[19] Bentley, I, 1–91 (the chapter entitled "The King's Company").

in the inner formes of sheets A, B, and I and in the outer formes of sheets D and K, among the copies collated. All variants, as concern substantive readings, are recorded in the textual notes.

STAGE HISTORY

The stage history of the play is worth noting. Information about seventeenth-century performances is meager, being confined to the statement on the quarto's title page that *The Broken Heart* had been acted by the King's company at Blackfriars. In 1668, during the Restoration, both *The Broken Heart* and *The Lover's Melancholy* were among the dramas allotted to D'Avenant's company, but there is no record that he ever staged them.[20] In 1898 *The Broken Heart* was produced by William Poel and in 1904 by the Mermaid Society, both performances being given in London.

More recently, in 1962, the play was produced by Sir Laurence Olivier at the Festival Theatre in Chichester. The cast included Sir Laurence as Bassanes, Rosemary Harris as Penthea, John Neville as Orgilus, Joan Greenwood as Calantha, and Keith Mitchell as Ithocles. According to the special correspondent for *The London Times*, Sir Laurence's Bassanes was "no comic stereotype but a strong courtier, fiercely jealous."[21] From the same viewer the role of Penthea received the most extended comment:

> Were Ford not the writer, Penthea might have been only a passive victim. What happens is that she refuses to escape, goes mad and dies, but not before she has rounded off her personality by forgiving Ithocles and pleading his cause to Calantha, the princess . . . . It [the role of Penthea] is in itself a good acting part and one could hope for few better interpreters than Miss Rosemary Harris. She bases her reading of it on the passionate love broken by her brother's decision. It bursts through the scene in which she dismisses her lover and conditions the poetic episode, which could have been a mere fading away, when her mind has cracked; and it is this experience of passion, thwarted or not, which prompts her generosity to the brother who is also her destroyer.[22]

[20] Allardyce Nicoll, *A History of Restoration Drama 1660–1700* (London, 1928), p. 315.
[21] See *The London Times*, July 10, 1962, p. 13.
[22] *Ibid.*

INTRODUCTION

To the Folger Shakespeare Library, where I spent the summer of 1965 on a fellowship grant, I wish to express my deepest thanks. Much of the research for this edition was done there, and was greatly facilitated by the fine staff of research assistants and librarians. I also am indebted to the Folger Library, the British Museum, the Yale Library, the Houghton Library, the Boston Public Library, and the University of Texas Library for Xerox reproductions of their copies of the 1633 quarto.

DONALD K. ANDERSON, JR.

University of Missouri

THE BROKEN HEART

To the Most Worthy Deserver of the Noblest Titles in Honor,
WILLIAM, LORD CRAVEN,
BARON OF HAMPSTEAD-MARSHALL

MY LORD:

The glory of a great name, acquired by a greater glory of   5
action, hath in all ages liv'd the truest chronicle to his own
memory. In the practice of which argument, your growth
to perfection (even in youth) hath appear'd so sincere, so
unflattering a penman, that posterity cannot with more
delight read the merit of noble endeavors, than noble   10
endeavors merit thanks from posterity to be read with
delight. Many nations, many eyes have been witnesses of
your deserts, and lov'd them. Be pleas'd, then, with the
freedom of your own nature, to admit one amongst all
particularly into the list of such as honor a fair example of   15
nobility. There is a kind of humble ambition, not uncom-
mendable, when the silence of study breaks forth into
discourse, coveting rather encouragement than applause;
yet herein censure commonly is too severe an auditor,
without the moderation of an able patronage. I have ever   20
been slow in courtship of greatness, not ignorant of such
defects as are frequent to opinion; but the justice of your
inclination to industry emboldens my weakness of confidence
to relish an experience of your mercy, as many brave
dangers have tasted of your courage. Your Lordship strove   25
to be known to the world (when the world knew you least)

---

2. *William, Lord Craven*] William, Lord Craven, eldest son of Sir William
Craven, Lord Mayor of London, lived from 1606 to 1697. Though enrolled
at Oxford, before he was twenty he entered the service of the Prince of
Orange and, gaining some military distinction, was in 1627 knighted, then
created Baron Craven of Hampstead-Marshall by Charles I. Supporting
the Elector Frederick and the Electress Elizabeth (daughter of James I)
in the Palatinate, in 1631 he was one of the commanders of English forces
in Germany, and was wounded at the taking of Creuznach. During the
Civil War and Commonwealth, he often provided financial assistance to the
widowed Elizabeth; however, the popular belief that they were secretly
married seems without foundation. In 1664 he was created Viscount
Craven of Uffington and Earl of Craven by Charles II (*DNB*).

9. *penman*] author.

−3−

by voluntary but excellent attempts. Like allowance I plead of being known to your Lordship (in this low presumption) by tend'ring, to a favorable entertainment, a devotion offer'd from a heart that can be as truly sensible 30 of any least respect as ever profess the owner in my best, my readiest services, a lover of your natural love to virtue,

JOHN FORD

---

29. *entertainment*] reception.

The scene, Sparta.

THE SPEAKERS' NAMES
fitted to their qualities.

AMYCLAS, *common to the kings of Laconia*
ITHOCLES, *Honor of Loveliness; a favorite*   5
ORGILUS, *Angry; son to Crotolon*
BASSANES, *Vexation; a jealous nobleman*
ARMOSTES, *an Appeaser; a councilor of state*
CROTOLON, *Noise; another councilor*
PROPHILUS, *Dear; friend to Ithocles*   10
NEARCHUS, *Young Prince; Prince of Argos*

---

1. *scene, Sparta*] S. P. Sherman ("Stella and the Broken Heart," *PMLA*, XXIV [1909], 275 ff.) believes Ford's Sparta to be modelled on that of Sidney's *Arcadia*; M. J. Sargeaunt (*John Ford* [Oxford, 1935], pp. 144–146) asserts that the Spartan setting is most fitting for the drama's characters, actions, and tone. It should be added that there is some historical context for the story, namely the three wars between Sparta and Messenia (743 to 453 B.C.); in the second scene of the first act, Ithocles returns as the conqueror of the Messenians.

2–3. *Speakers' ... qualities*] Gifford's comment, which never has been questioned, is uncomplimentary: "If he [Ford] found them [the names] elsewhere, it is well; if not, he has not been very successful in his appropriation of some of them." His comment also is unjust: in most cases, a character's name clearly has been derived from a Greek word designating his or her "quality" (see notes below). The three exceptions to this procedure seem to be *Amyclas, Ithocles,* and *Amelus. Amyclas* Ford may have obtained from the history of Pausanias (Bk. III, Ch. I), who mentions a legendary figure of that name who was the son of Lacedemon and Sparta and who built the city of Amyclae; another possible source (pointed out by Sherman) is Sidney's *Arcadia*, which has a Spartan king named Amyclas. *Ithocles* and *Amelus* have no apparent derivations. The stronghold of the Messenians during their wars with Sparta was called Ithome (cited by most Greek historians), but it is not mentioned in the play.

6. *Orgilus, Angry*] from ὀργίλος, meaning "inclined to anger" (*L and S*).

7. *Bassanes, Vexation*] from ἡ βᾰσάνος, meaning "a trial or test" (*L and S*).

8. *Armostes, an Appeaser*] from ὁ ἅρμοστής, meaning "one who arranges or governs" (*L and S*). Of the same origin is the current English word *harmost*, meaning "a governor appointed by the Spartans over subject towns and people"; at the end of the play, Armostes is appointed viceroy of Argos.

9. *Crotolon, Noise*] from ὁ κρότος, meaning "a rattling noise" (*L and S*).

10. *Prophilus, Dear*] probably derived from combining φίλος, meaning "dear," and the prefix προ, meaning "before" (*L and S*).

11. *Nearchus, Young Prince*] from the prefix νε, meaning "fresh, young," and ὁ ἀρχός, meaning "leader, chief" (*L and S*).

TECNICUS, *Artist; a philosopher*
HEMOPHIL, *Glutton;*
GRONEAS, *Tavern-haunter;* } *two courtiers*
AMELUS, *Trusty; friend to Nearchus*   15
PHULAS, *Watchful; servant to Bassanes*

CALANTHA, *Flower of Beauty; the king's daughter*
PENTHEA, *Complaint; sister to Ithocles*
EUPHRANEA, *Joy; a maid of honor*
CHRISTALLA, *Crystal;*
PHILEMA, *a Kiss;* } *maids of honor*   20
GRAUSIS, *Old Beldam; overseer of Penthea*

Persons included

THRASUS, *Fierceness; father of Ithocles*
APLOTES, *Simplicity; Orgilus so disguis'd*   25

[Attendants, Servants, Singers]

13. HEMOPHIL] *Weber;* Lemophil   *of sheet K.*
Q. Hemophil *used elsewhere through-*   22. GRAUSIS] *Q (corr.)*; Gransis *Q*
out Q except for inner and outer formes   *(uncorr.)*. Gransis *used throughout Q*.

---

12. *Tecnicus, Artist*] from τεχνικός, meaning "artistic" (*L and S*).

13. *Hemophil, Glutton*] apparently derived from combining τό αἷμα, meaning "blood," and φίλος, meaning "fond of" (*L and S*), though "blood-lover" and "glutton" hardly are synonymous. *Hemophil* may refer to the bravado of this braggart soldier (I.ii).

14. *Groneas, Tavern-haunter*] possibly from γρῶνος, meaning "eaten out, cavernous, hollow," or from ἡ γρῶνη, meaning "hole, or hollow vessel" (*L and S*).

16. *Phulas, Watchful*] from φυλάσσω, meaning "to keep watch and ward, especially by night" (*L and S*)—precisely Phulas' responsibility concerning Penthea.

17. *Calantha, Flower of Beauty*] from τό κάλλος, meaning "beauty," and ἡ ἄνθη, meaning "full bloom of a flower or plant" (*L and S*).

18. *Penthea, Complaint*] from πενθέω, meaning "to mourn, lament" (*L and S*).

19. *Euphranea, Joy*] from ὁ εὐφράντης, meaning "one who cheers, gladdens" (*L and S*).

20. *Christalla, Crystal*] from ὁ κρύσταλλος, meaning "ice, crystal" (*L and S*).

21. *Philema, a Kiss*] from τό φίλημα, meaning "a kiss" (*L and S*).

22. *Grausis, Old Beldam*] from ἡ γραῦς, meaning "old woman" (*L and S*), which is the meaning of *beldam*.

23. *Persons included*] This addition to the list of dramatis personae is unusual, one name being that of a person dead before the play begins and the other that assumed by a character in disguise.

24. *Thrasus, Fierceness*] from θρᾰσύς, meaning "bold" (*L and S*).

25. *Aplotes, Simplicity*] from ἡ ἁπλότης, meaning "simplicity" (*L and S*).

THE PROLOGUE

Our scene is Sparta. He whose best of art
Hath drawn this piece calls it *The Broken Heart*.
The title lends no expectation here
Of apish laughter or of some lame jeer
At place or persons; no pretended clause   5
Of jests fit for a brothel courts applause
From vulgar admiration. Such low songs,
Tun'd to unchaste ears, suit not modest tongues.
The Virgin Sisters then deserv'd fresh bays
When innocence and sweetness crown'd their lays;   10
Then vices gasp'd for breath, whose whole commerce
Was whipp'd to exile by unblushing verse.
This law we keep in our presentment now,
Not to take freedom more than we allow.
What may be here thought a fiction, when time's youth   15
Wanted some riper years was known a truth;
In which, if words have cloth'd the subject right,
You may partake a pity with delight.

---

4. *apish*] given to servile imitation.
9. *Virgin Sisters*] the Muses.
9. *bays*] bay leaves, a token of honor.
16. *Wanted*] lacked.

The Broken Heart

Enter Crotolon *and* Orgilus.

CROTOLON.

    Dally not further; I will know the reason
    That speeds thee to this journey.

ORGILUS.   Reason? Good sir,

    I can yield many.

CROTOLON.   Give me one, a good one;

    Such I expect, and ere we part must have.
    Athens? Pray why to Athens? You intend not   5
    To kick against the world, turn cynic, stoic,
    Or read the logic lecture, or become
    An Areopagite, and judge in causes
    Touching the commonwealth? For as I take it,
    The budding of your chin cannot prognosticate   10
    So grave an honor.

ORGILUS.   All this I acknowledge.

CROTOLON.

    You do? Then, son, if books and love of knowledge
    Inflame you to this travel, here in Sparta
    You may as freely study.

ORGILUS.   'Tis not that, sir.

CROTOLON.

    Not that, sir? As a father I command thee   15
    To acquaint me with the truth.

ORGILUS.   Thus I obey 'ee.

    After so many quarrels as dissension,
    Fury, and rage had broach'd in blood, and sometimes
    With death to such confederates as sided
    With now-dead Thrasus and yourself my lord,   20

18. broach'd] *Weber;* brauch't *Q.*

---

8. *Areopagite*] a member of the Areopagus, the famous Athenian court.

Our present king, Amyclas, reconcil'd
Your eager swords and seal'd a gentle peace.
Friends you profess'd yourselves, which to confirm,
A resolution for a lasting league
Betwixt your families was entertain'd,   25
By joining in a Hymenean bond
Me and the fair Penthea, only daughter
To Thrasus.

CROTOLON.   What of this?

ORGILUS.   Much, much, dear sir.
A freedom of converse, an interchange
Of holy and chaste love, so fix'd our souls   30
In a firm growth of union, that no time
Can eat into the pledge; we had enjoy'd
The sweets our vows expected, had not cruelty
Prevented all those triumphs we prepar'd for,
By Thrasus his untimely death.

CROTOLON.   Most certain.   35

ORGILUS.
From this time sprouted up that poisonous stalk
Of aconite, whose ripened fruit hath ravish'd
All health, all comfort of a happy life.
For Ithocles her brother, proud of youth,
And prouder in his power, nourish'd closely   40
The memory of former discontents.
To glory in revenge, by cunning partly,
Partly by threats, 'a woos at once and forces
His virtuous sister to admit a marriage
With Bassanes, a nobleman, in honor   45
And riches, I confess, beyond my fortunes.

CROTOLON.
All this is no sound reason to importune

---

21. reconcil'd] *Q* (*corr.*); recoacil'd   31. of union] *Q* (*corr.*); of holy
Q (*uncorr.*).   union *Q* (*uncorr.*).

---

26. *Hymenean bond*] marriage.
37. *aconite*] a poisonous plant; here probably the species also called
monkshood or wolfsbane.
40. *closely*] secretly.
43. *'a*] he.
44. *admit*] consent to.

My leave for thy departure.

ORGILUS.   Now it follows.
Beauteous Penthea, wedded to this torture
By an insulting brother, being secretly   50
Compell'd to yield her virgin freedom up
To him who never can usurp her heart
Before contracted mine, is now so yok'd
To a most barbarous thralldom, misery,
Affliction, that he savors not humanity   55
Whose sorrow melts not into more than pity
In hearing but her name.

CROTOLON.   As how, pray?

ORGILUS.   Bassanes,
The man that calls her wife, considers truly
What heaven of perfections he is lord of,
By thinking fair Penthea his. This thought   60
Begets a kind of monster-love, which love
Is nurse unto a fear so strong and servile
As brands all dotage with a jealousy.
All eyes who gaze upon that shrine of beauty,
He doth resolve, do homage to the miracle;   65
Someone, he is assur'd, may now or then,
If opportunity but sort, prevail.
So much out of a self-unworthiness
His fears transport him, not that he finds cause
In her obedience, but his own distrust.   70

CROTOLON.
You spin out your discourse.

ORGILUS.   My griefs are violent.
For knowing how the maid was heretofore
Courted by me, his jealousies grow wild
That I should steal again into her favors,
And undermine her virtues, which the gods   75
Know I nor dare nor dream of. Hence, from hence
I undertake a voluntary exile.
First, by my absence to take off the cares

---

50. *insulting*] arrogant.
65. *resolve*] conclude.
67. *sort*] come about.

Of jealous Bassanes, but chiefly, sir,
To free Penthea from a hell on earth.   80
Lastly, to lose the memory of something
Her presence makes to live in me afresh.

CROTOLON.

Enough, my Orgilus, enough. To Athens,
I give a full consent. —Alas good lady!—
We shall hear from thee often?

ORGILUS.   Often.

CROTOLON.   See,   85
Thy sister comes to give a farewell.

Enter Euphranea.

EUPHRANEA.   Brother.

ORGILUS.

Euphranea, thus upon thy cheeks I print
A brother's kiss, more careful of thine honor,
Thy health, and thy well-doing than my life.
Before we part, in presence of our father   90
I must prefer a suit to 'ee.

EUPHRANEA.   You may style it,
My brother, a command.

ORGILUS.   That you will promise
To pass never to any man, however
Worthy, your faith, till with our father's leave
I give a free consent.

CROTOLON.   An easy motion.   95
I'll promise for her, Orgilus.

ORGILUS.   Your pardon;
Euphranea's oath must yield me satisfaction.

EUPHRANEA.

By Vesta's sacred fires I swear.

CROTOLON.   And I
By great Apollo's beams join in the vow,

---

91. *prefer*] present.
91. *'ee*] ye.
95. *motion*] proposal.
98. *Vesta's sacred fires*] The altar of Vesta, Roman goddess of the hearth,
was attended by virgins.

Not without thy allowance to bestow her   100
On any living.

ORGILUS.   Dear Euphranea,
Mistake me not; far, far 'tis from my thought,
As far from any wish of mine, to hinder
Preferment to an honorable bed
Or fitting fortune. Thou art young and handsome;   105
And 'twere injustice, more, a tyranny,
Not to advance thy merit. Trust me, sister,
It shall be my first care to see thee match'd
As may become thy choice and our contents.
I have your oath.

EUPHRANEA.   You have. But mean you, brother,   110
To leave us as you say?

CROTOLON.   Ay, ay, Euphranea;
He has just grounds direct him. I will prove
A father and a brother to thee.

EUPHRANEA.   Heaven
Does look into the secrets of all hearts.
Gods, you have mercy with 'ee, else—

CROTOLON.   Doubt nothing   115
Thy brother will return in safety to us.

ORGILUS.
Souls sunk in sorrows never are without 'em;
They change fresh airs, but bear their griefs about 'em.

Exeunt omnes.

[I.ii]

Flourish. Enter Amyclas *the king*, Armostes, Prophilus, *and attendants.*

AMYCLAS.
The Spartan gods are gracious. Our humility
Shall bend before their altars, and perfume
Their temples with abundant sacrifice.
See lords, Amyclas your old king is ent'ring
Into his youth again. I shall shake off   5

111. Ay, ay] *Gifford;* I, I *Q.*

---

109. *contents*] satisfaction.
115. *Doubt nothing*] Doubt not.

This silver badge of age, and change this snow
For hairs as gay as are Apollo's locks;
Our heart leaps in new vigor.

ARMOSTES.   May old time
Run back to double your long life, great sir.

AMYCLAS.
It will, it must, Armostes. Thy bold nephew,   10
Death-braving Ithocles, brings to our gates
Triumphs and peace upon his conquering sword.
Laconia is a monarchy at length,
Hath in this latter war trod underfoot
Messene's pride; Messene bows her neck   15
To Lacedemon's royalty. O, 'twas
A glorious victory, and doth deserve
More than a chronicle: a temple, lords,
A temple to the name of Ithocles.—
Where didst thou leave him, Prophilus?

PROPHILUS.   At Pephon,   20
Most gracious sovereign; twenty of the noblest
Of the Messenians there attend your pleasure
For such conditions as you shall propose,
In settling peace and liberty of life.

AMYCLAS.
When comes your friend the general?

PROPHILUS.   He promis'd   25
To follow with all speed convenient.

Enter Crotolon, Calantha, Christalla, Philema, *and* Euphranea.

AMYCLAS.
Our daughter. —Dear Calantha, the happy news,
The conquest of Messene, hath already
Enrich'd thy knowledge.

CALANTHA.   With the circumstance

---

13. *Laconia*] southeastern part of Peloponnesus; its capital was Sparta.

15. *Messene*] "The town of this name was not founded till after the overthrow of the Spartan supremacy, but the name was anciently given to
Messenia" (Spencer). Messenia was northwest of Laconia.

16. *Lacedemon*] another name for Sparta.

20. *Pephon*] Pephnus, a Laconian town near Messene.

And manner of the fight, related faithfully   30
By Prophilus himself; but pray sir, tell me,
How doth the youthful general demean
His actions in these fortunes?

PROPHILUS.   Excellent princess,
Your own fair eyes may soon report a truth
Unto your judgment, with what moderation,   35
Calmness of nature, measure, bounds, and limits
Of thankfulness and joy 'a doth digest
Such amplitude of his success as would
In others, molded of a spirit less clear,
Advance 'em to comparison with heaven.   40
But Ithocles—

CALANTHA.   Your friend—

PROPHILUS.   He is so, madam,
In which the period of my fate consists.
He in this firmament of honor stands
Like a star fix'd, not mov'd with any thunder
Of popular applause, or sudden lightning   45
Of self-opinion. He hath serv'd his country,
And thinks 'twas but his duty.

CROTOLON.   You describe
A miracle of man.

AMYCLAS.   Such, Crotolon,
On forfeit of a king's word, thou wilt find him.—
Hark, warning of his coming. All attend him.   50

Flourish. Enter Ithocles, Hemophil, *and* Groneas, *the rest of the lords
ushering him in.*

AMYCLAS.
Return into these arms, thy home, thy sanctuary,
Delight of Sparta, treasure of my bosom,
Mine own, own Ithocles.

ITHOCLES.   Your humblest subject.

ARMOSTES.
Proud of the blood I claim an interest in
As brother to thy mother, I embrace thee,   55
Right noble nephew.

---

42. *period*] summation.

ITHOCLES.   Sir, your love's too partial.

CROTOLON.

Our country speaks by me, who by thy valor,
Wisdom, and service shares in this great action,
Returning thee, in part of thy due merits,
A general welcome.

ITHOCLES.   You exceed in bounty.   60

CALANTHA.

Christalla, Philema, the chaplet. —Ithocles,
Upon the wings of fame the singular
And chosen fortune of an high attempt
Is borne so past the view of common sight
That I myself, with mine own hands, have wrought   65
To crown thy temples this provincial garland;
Accept, wear, and enjoy it as our gift
Deserv'd, not purchas'd.

ITHOCLES.   Y'are a royal maid.

AMYCLAS.

She is in all our daughter.

ITHOCLES.   Let me blush,
Acknowledging how poorly I have serv'd,   70
What nothings I have done, compar'd with th' honors
Heap'd on the issue of a willing mind;
In that lay mine ability, that only.
For who is he so sluggish from his birth,
So little worthy of a name or country,   75
That owes not out of gratitude for life
A debt of service, in what kind soever
Safety or counsel of the commonwealth
Requires for payment?

CALANTHA.   'A speaks truth.

ITHOCLES.   Whom heaven
Is pleas'd to style victorious, there, to such,   80
Applause runs madding, like the drunken priests
In Bacchus' sacrifices, without reason
Voicing the leader-on a demigod,

---

59. *in part*] on behalf.   61. *chaplet*] garland.
66. *provincial garland*] "the wreath (of laurel) ... which the ancients
conferred on those who ... had added a *province* to the empire" (Gifford).

Whenas indeed each common soldier's blood
Drops down as current coin in that hard purchase   85
As his whose much more delicate condition
Hath suck'd the milk of ease. Judgment commands,
But resolution executes. I use not,
Before this royal presence, these fit slights
As in contempt of such as can direct.   90
My speech hath other end, not to attribute
All praise to one man's fortune, which is strengthed
By many hands. For instance, here is Prophilus,
A gentleman (I cannot flatter truth)
Of much desert; and, though in other rank,   95
Both Hemophil and Groneas were not missing
To wish their country's peace. For in a word,
All there did strive their best, and 'twas our duty.

AMYCLAS.

Courtiers turn soldiers? —We vouchsafe our hand.
Observe your great example.

HEMOPHIL.   With all diligence.   100

GRONEAS.

Obsequiously and hourly.

AMYCLAS.   Some repose
After these toils are needful. We must think on
Conditions for the conquered; they expect 'em.
On. —Come, my Ithocles.

EUPHRANEA.   Sir, with your favor,
I need not a supporter.

PROPHILUS.   Fate instructs me.   105

Exeunt. Manent Hemophil, Groneas, Christalla, *et* Philema. Hemophil
stays Christalla; Groneas, Philema.

CHRISTALLA.

With me?

PHILEMA.   Indeed I dare not stay.

HEMOPHIL.   Sweet lady,

---

89. *fit slights*] "i.e., these appropriate depreciatory expressions" (Spencer).
100. *Observe*] pay respect to.
103. *expect*] await.
105.1. *Manent*] remain.

Soldiers are blunt—your lip.

CHRISTALLA.   Fie, this is rudeness;
  You went not hence such creatures.

GRONEAS.   Spirit of valor
  Is of a mounting nature.

PHILEMA.   It appears so.
  Pray in earnest, how many men apiece   110
  Have you two been the death of?

GRONEAS.   Faith not many;
  We were compos'd of mercy.

HEMOPHIL.   For our daring
  You heard the general's approbation
  Before the king.

CHRISTALLA.   You wish'd your country's peace;
  That showed your charity. Where are your spoils,   115
  Such as the soldier fights for?

PHILEMA.   They are coming.

CHRISTALLA.
  By the next carrier, are they not?

GRONEAS.   Sweet Philema,
  When I was in the thickest of mine enemies,
  Slashing off one man's head, another's nose,
  Another's arms and legs—

PHILEMA.   And all together—   120

GRONEAS.
  Then would I with a sigh remember thee,
  And cry, "Dear Philema, 'tis for thy sake
  I do these deeds of wonder!" Dost not love me
  With all thy heart now?

PHILEMA.   Now as heretofore.
  I have not put my love to use; the principal   125
  Will hardly yield an interest.

GRONEAS.   By Mars,
  I'll marry thee.

PHILEMA.   By Vulcan, y'are forsworn,

111. you] *Weber;* yon *Q.*

---

125. *to use*] out at interest.

127. *Vulcan*] "The husband of Venus who trapped her in the act of adultery with Mars" (Harrier).

127. *forsworn*] perjured.

Except my mind do alter strangely.

GRONEAS.   One word.

CHRISTALLA.

You lie beyond all modesty. Forbear me.

HEMOPHIL.

I'll make thee mistress of a city; 'tis   130
Mine own by conquest.

CHRISTALLA.   By petition; sue for 't
In forma pauperis. City? Kennel. Gallants,
Off with your feathers; put on aprons, gallants.
Learn to reel, thrum, or trim a lady's dog,
And be good, quiet souls of peace, hobgoblins.   135

HEMOPHIL.

Christalla!

CHRISTALLA.   Practice to drill hogs, in hope
To share in the acorns. Soldiers? Corn-cutters,
But not so valiant. They ofttimes draw blood,
Which you durst never do. When you have practic'd
More wit or more civility, we'll rank 'ee   140
I'th' list of men. Till then, brave things-at-arms,
Dare not to speak to us—most potent Groneas.

PHILEMA.

And Hemophil the hardy—at your services.

GRONEAS.

They scorn us as they did before we went.

HEMOPHIL.

Hang 'em, let us scorn them and be reveng'd.   145

                                   Exeunt Christalla *et* Philema.

GRONEAS.

Shall we?

HEMOPHIL.   We will; and when we slight them thus

133. feathers] *Weber;* Fathers *Q.*

---

132. *In . . . pauperis*] as a pauper.
132. *Kennel*] gutter.
133. *aprons*] workingmen's clothes.
134. *reel*] wind cloth or thread.
134. *thrum*] "Weave. Thrum is, properly, the tuft at the end of the warp" (Ellis).
136–137. *drill . . . acorns*] proverbial; cf. Tilley, H 492.
137. *Corn-cutters*] those who cut corns on the feet, chiropodists.

Instead of following them, they'll follow us.
It is a woman's nature.

GRONEAS.   'Tis a scurvy one.   *Exeunt omnes.*

[I.iii]
Enter Tecnicus, *a philosopher; and* Orgilus *disguised like a scholar of his.*

TECNICUS.

> Tempt not the stars, young man; thou canst not play
> With the severity of fate. This change
> Of habit, and disguise in outward view,
> Hides not the secrets of thy soul within thee
> From their quick-piercing eyes, which dive at all times   5
> Down to thy thoughts. In thy aspect I note
> A consequence of danger.

ORGILUS.   Give me leave,

> Grave Tecnicus, without foredooming destiny,
> Under thy roof to ease my silent griefs
> By applying to my hidden wounds the balm   10
> Of thy oraculous lectures. If my fortune
> Run such a crooked byway as to wrest
> My steps to ruin, yet thy learned precepts
> Shall call me back and set my footings straight.
> I will not court the world.

TECNICUS.   Ah Orgilus,   15

> Neglects in young men of delights and life
> Run often to extremities; they care not
> For harms to others who contemn their own.

ORGILUS.

> But I, most learned artist, am not so much
> At odds with nature that I grutch the thrift   20
> Of any true deserver. Nor doth malice
> Of present hopes so check them with despair,
> As that I yield to thought of more affliction

---

3. *habit*] apparel.

8. *foredooming*] "That is, pre-judging the fate of Orgilus as an evil one" (Harrier).

20. *grutch*] grudge.   20. *thrift*] success.

21–22. *malice . . . hopes*] i.e., "the misfortunes which my present hopes have met" (Sherman).

Than what is incident to frailty. Wherefore
Impute not this retired course of living   25
Some little time to any other cause
Than what I justly render: the information
Of an unsettled mind, as the effect
Must clearly witness.
TECNICUS.   Spirit of truth inspire thee.
On these conditions I conceal thy change,   30
And willingly admit thee for an auditor.
I'll to my study.
ORGILUS.   I to contemplations
In these delightful walks.—   [*Exit* Tecnicus.]
                        Thus metamorphos'd,
I may without suspicion harken after
Penthea's usage and Euphranea's faith.   35
Love, thou art full of mystery! The deities
Themselves are not secure in searching out
The secrets of those flames, which hidden waste
A breast made tributary to the laws
Of beauty; physic yet hath never found   40
A remedy to cure a lover's wound.
Ha! Who are those that cross yon private walk
Into the shadowing grove in amorous foldings?

Prophilus *passeth over, supporting* Euphranea, *and whispering.*

My sister; O, my sister! 'Tis Euphranea
With Prophilus; supported too. I would   45
It were an apparition. Prophilus
Is Ithocles his friend. It strangely puzzles me.
Again? Help me, my book; this scholar's habit
Must stand my privilege. My mind is busy,
Mine eyes and ears are open.   *Walk by, reading.*

Enter again Prophilus *and* Euphranea.

PROPHILUS.   Do not waste   50
The span of this stol'n time (lent by the gods

---

31. *auditor*] student.
49. *stand my privilege*] i.e., constitute my right to be here.

For precious use) in niceness. Bright Euphranea,
Should I repeat old vows, or study new,
For purchase of belief to my desires—
ORGILUS [*aside*].
   Desires?
PROPHILUS.   My service, my integrity—   55
ORGILUS [*aside*].
   That's better.
PROPHILUS.   I should but repeat a lesson
Oft conn'd without a prompter but thine eyes.
My love is honorable.
ORGILUS [*aside*].   So was mine
To my Penthea; chastely honorable.
PROPHILUS.
Nor wants there more addition to my wish   60
Of happiness than having thee a wife,
Already sure of Ithocles, a friend
Firm and unalterable.
ORGILUS [*aside*].   But a brother
More cruel than the grave.
EUPHRANEA.   What can you look for
In answer to your noble protestations,   65
From an unskillful maid, but language suited
To a divided mind?
ORGILUS [*aside*].   Hold out, Euphranea!
EUPHRANEA.
Know Prophilus, I never undervalued
(From the first time you mentioned worthy love)
Your merit, means, or person. It had been   70
A fault of judgment in me, and a dullness
In my affections, not to weigh and thank
My better stars, that offered me the grace
Of so much blissfulness. For to speak truth,
The law of my desires kept equal pace   75
With yours, nor have I left that resolution;
But only in a word, whatever choice
Lives nearest in my heart must first procure
Consent both from my father and my brother,

---

52. *niceness*] coyness.

Ere he can own me his.

ORGILUS [*aside*].   She is forsworn else.   80

PROPHILUS.

    Leave me that task.

EUPHRANEA.   My brother, ere he parted
    To Athens, had my oath.

ORGILUS [*aside*].   Yes, yes, 'a had sure.

PROPHILUS.

    I doubt not, with the means the court supplies,
    But to prevail at pleasure.

ORGILUS [*aside*].   Very likely.

PROPHILUS.

    Meantime, best, dearest, I may build my hopes   85
    On the foundation of thy constant suff'rance
    In any opposition.

EUPHRANEA.   Death shall sooner
    Divorce life and the joys I have in living,
    Than my chaste vows from truth.

PROPHILUS.   On thy fair hand
    I seal the like.

ORGILUS [*aside*].   There is no faith in woman.   90
    Passion, O, be contain'd! My very heartstrings
    Are on the tenters.

EUPHRANEA.   Sir, we are overheard.
    Cupid protect us! 'Twas a stirring, sir,
    Of someone near.

PROPHILUS.   Your fears are needless, lady;
    None have access into these private pleasures   95
    Except some near in court, or bosom student
    From Tecnicus his oratory, granted
    By special favor lately from the king
    Unto the grave philosopher.

EUPHRANEA.   Methinks
    I hear one talking to himself. I see him.   100

PROPHILUS.

    'Tis a poor scholar, as I told you, lady.

---

    86. *constant suff'rance*] loyal endurance, steadfastness.

    87. *In*] in case of.

    92. *tenters*] "frames with hooks on which cloth is hung after having been dyed" (Weber).

    97. *oratory*] lecture hall.

ORGILUS [*aside*].

    I am discovered.— [*As if studying aloud.*]
                  Say it: is it possible
    With a smooth tongue, a leering countenance,
    Flattery, or force of reason—I come t'ee, sir—
    To turn or to appease the raging sea?   105
    Answer to that. Your art? What art to catch
    And hold fast in a net the sun's small atoms?
    No, no; they'll out, they'll out; ye may as easily
    Outrun a cloud driven by a northern blast
    As fiddle-faddle so. Peace, or speak sense.   110

EUPHRANEA.

    Call you this thing a scholar? 'Las, he's lunatic.

PROPHILUS.

    Observe him, sweet; 'tis but his recreation.

ORGILUS.

    But will you hear a little? You are so tetchy,
    You keep no rule in argument. Philosophy
    Works not upon impossibilities   115
    But natural conclusions. Mew? Absurd.
    The metaphysics are but speculations
    Of the celestial bodies or such accidents
    As not mixt perfectly, in the air engender'd,
    Appear to us unnatural; that's all.   120
    Prove it; yet with a reverence to your gravity,
    I'll balk illiterate sauciness, submitting
    My sole opinion to the touch of writers.

PROPHILUS.

    Now let us fall in with him.

ORGILUS.   Ha, ha, ha!
    These apish boys, when they but taste the grammates   125
    And principles of theory, imagine
    They can oppose their teachers. Confidence

---

   113. *tetchy*] irritable.
   116. *Mew*] an exclamation of contempt.
   117. *speculations*] (1) opinions; (2) observations of the heavens, stars.
   118. *accidents*] "That is, not substances, in Aristotelian philosophy" (Harrier).
   123. *touch*] test.
   125. *grammates*] rudiments.

Leads many into errors.

PROPHILUS.   By your leave, sir.

EUPHRANEA.

    Are you a scholar, friend?

ORGILUS.   I am, gay creature,

    With pardon of your deities, a mushroom   130
    On whom the dew of heaven drops now and then.
    The sun shines on me too, I thank his beams;
    Sometime I feel their warmth, and eat and sleep.

PROPHILUS.

    Does Tecnicus read to thee?

ORGILUS.   Yes forsooth,

    He is my master surely; yonder door   135
    Opens upon his study.

PROPHILUS.   Happy creatures.

    Such people toil not, sweet, in heats of state,
    Nor sink in thaws of greatness. Their affections
    Keep order with the limits of their modesty.
    Their love is love of virtue. —What's thy name?   140

ORGILUS.

    Aplotes, sumptuous master, a poor wretch.

EUPHRANEA.

    Dost thou want anything?

ORGILUS.   Books, Venus, books.

PROPHILUS.

    Lady, a new conceit comes in my thought,
    And most available for both our comforts.

EUPHRANEA.

    My lord—

PROPHILUS.   Whiles I endeavor to deserve   145
    Your father's blessing to our loves, this scholar
    May daily at some certain hours attend
    What notice I can write of my success,
    Here in this grove, and give it to your hands;
    The like from you to me. So can we never,   150
    Barr'd of our mutual speech, want sure intelligence,
    And thus our hearts may talk when our tongues cannot.

---

134. *read to*] teach.   139. *modesty*] moderation.
143. *conceit*] idea, thought.   147. *attend*] wait for.

EUPHRANEA.

    Occasion is most favorable; use it.

PROPHILUS.

    Aplotes, wilt thou wait us twice a day,
    At nine i'th' morning and at four at night,   155
    Here in this bower, to convey such letters
    As each shall send to other? Do it willingly,
    Safely, and secretly, and I will furnish
    Thy study or what else thou canst desire.

ORGILUS.

    Jove, make me thankful, thankful, I beseech thee,   160
    Propitious Jove. I will prove sure and trusty.
    You will not fail me books?

PROPHILUS.   Nor aught besides
    Thy heart can wish. This lady's name's Euphranea,
    Mine Prophilus.

ORGILUS.   I have a pretty memory;
    It must prove my best friend. I will not miss   165
    One minute of the hours appointed.

PROPHILUS.   Write
    The books thou wouldst have bought thee in a note,
    Or take thyself some money.

ORGILUS.   No, no money.
    Money to scholars is a spirit invisible;
    We dare not finger it. Or books or nothing.   170

PROPHILUS.

    Books of what sort thou wilt. Do not forget
    Our names.

ORGILUS.   I warrant 'ee, I warrant 'ee.

PROPHILUS.

    Smile, Hymen, on the growth of our desires;
    We'll feed thy torches with eternal fires.

Exeunt. Manet Orgilus.

ORGILUS.

    Put out thy torches, Hymen, or their light   175

---

   164. *pretty*] fine, excellent.

   170. *Or*] either.

   173. *Hymen*] the god of marriage, represented as carrying a bridal
torch.

Shall meet a darkness of eternal night.
Inspire me, Mercury, with swift deceits;
Ingenious fate has leapt into mine arms,
Beyond the compass of my brain. Mortality
Creeps on the dung of earth and cannot reach   180
The riddles which are purpos'd by the gods.
Great arts best write themselves in their own stories;
They die too basely who outlive their glories.   *Exit.*

[II.i]   *Enter* Bassanes *and* Phulas.

BASSANES.

I'll have that window next the street damm'd up;
It gives too full a prospect to temptation,
And courts a gazer's glances. There's a lust
Committed by the eye, that sweats and travails,
Plots, wakes, contrives, till the deformed bear-whelp   5
Adultery be lick'd into the act,
The very act. That light shall be damm'd up;
D'ee hear, sir?
PHULAS.   I do hear, my lord; a mason
Shall be provided suddenly.
BASSANES.   Some rogue,
Some rogue of your confederacy, factor   10
For slaves and strumpets, to convey close packets
From this spruce springal and the tother youngster,
That gaudy earwig, or my lord your patron,
Whose pensioner you are. I'll tear thy throat out,
Son of a cat, ill-looking hound's-head, rip up   15
Thy ulcerous maw, if I but scent a paper,
A scroll, but half as big as what can cover

---

1. *I'll . . . up*] In this scene the symptoms of Bassanes' jealousy probably
are taken from Burton. Cf. *The Anatomy of Melancholy*, Part. 3, Sect. 3,
Memb. 2.

5–6. *deformed . . . lick'd*] An ancient belief held that the mother bear
shapes or forms her newly-born whelps by licking them. Cf. Pliny, VIII.liv.

10. *factor*] agent.

11. *close packets*] secret letters.

12. *springal*] youth.

13. *earwig*] a whispering busybody (named after the insect that supposedly
creeps into a person's ear).

A wart upon thy nose, a spot, a pimple,
Directed to my lady. It may prove
A mystical preparative to lewdness.   20

PHULAS.

Care shall be had. I will turn every thread
About me to an eye. —[*Aside.*]   Here's a sweet life!

BASSANES.

The city housewives, cunning in the traffic
Of chamber merchandise, set all at price
By wholesale, yet they wipe their mouths, and simper,   25
Cull, kiss, and cry "sweetheart," and stroke the head
Which they have branch'd, and all is well again.
Dull clods of dirt, who dare not feel the rubs
Stuck on the foreheads.

PHULAS.   'Tis a villainous world;
One cannot hold his own in't.

BASSANES.   Dames at court,   30
Who flaunt in riots, run another bias.
Their pleasure heaves the patient ass that suffers
Up on the stilts of office, titles, incomes;
Promotion justifies the shame, and sues for't.
Poor honor, thou art stabb'd, and bleed'st to death   35
By such unlawful hire! The country mistress
Is yet more wary, and in blushes hides
Whatever trespass draws her troth to guilt;
But all are false. On this truth I am bold:
No woman but can fall, and doth, or would.—   40
Now for the newest news about the city;
What blab the voices, sirrah?

PHULAS.   O, my lord,

---

26. *Cull*] embrace.

26–27. *head . . . branch'd*] "an allusion to the familiar notion that horns
grow on the forehead of a man whose wife has been unfaithful to him"
(Sherman).

28. *rubs*] (1) impediments, hindrances; (2) reproofs.

31. *riots*] profligate or extravagant living.

31. *bias*] direction; like *rubs* (1), a bowling term: "'Twill make me think
the world is full of rubs,/ And that my fortune runs against the bias"
(*Richard II*, III.iv.5–6).

42. *sirrah*] "a term of address used to men or boys, expressing contempt,
reprimand, or assumption of authority on the part of the speaker" (*OED*).

−27−

The rarest, quaintest, strangest, tickling news
That ever—
BASSANES.   Heyday, up and ride me, rascal!
What is't?
PHULAS.   Forsooth, they say the king has mew'd   45
All his gray beard, instead of which is budded
Another of a pure carnation color
Speckled with green and russet.
BASSANES.   Ignorant block!
PHULAS.
Yes truly, and 'tis talk'd about the streets
That, since Lord Ithocles came home, the lions   50
Never left roaring, at which noise the bears
Have danc'd their very hearts out.
BASSANES.   Dance out thine too.
PHULAS.
Besides, Lord Orgilus is fled to Athens
Upon a fiery dragon, and 'tis thought
'A never can return.
BASSANES.   Grant it, Apollo.   55
PHULAS.
Moreover, please your lordship, 'tis reported
For certain that whoever is found jealous
Without apparent proof that 's wife is wanton,
Shall be divorc'd. But this is but she-news,
I had it from a midwife. I have more yet.   60
BASSANES.
Antic, no more; idiots and stupid fools
Grate my calamities. Why to be fair
Should yield presumption of a faulty soul?
Look to the doors.
PHULAS [aside].   The horn of plenty crest him.   Exit Phulas.

---

44. *Heyday*] "an exclamation denoting frolicsomeness, gaiety, surprise, wonder" (*OED*).

45. *mew'd*] "falconer's language . . . . To mew, or rather mue, is to moult, to shed feathers" (Gifford).

61. *Antic*] fool.

63. *yield presumption*] arouse suspicion.

64. *horn of plenty*] "cornucopia; but allusive to the horns of a cuckold" (Spencer).

BASSANES.

    Swarms of confusion huddle in my thoughts   65
    In rare distemper. Beauty! O, it is
    An unmatch'd blessing or a horrid curse.

       Enter Penthea *and* Grausis, *an old lady.*

    She comes, she comes. So shoots the morning forth,
    Spangled with pearls of transparent dew.
    The way to poverty is to be rich;   70
    As I in her am wealthy, but for her
    In all contents a bankrupt. —Lov'd Penthea,
    How fares my heart's best joy?

GRAUSIS.   In sooth not well,
    She is so oversad.

BASSANES.   Leave chattering, magpie.—
    Thy brother is return'd, sweet, safe and honor'd   75
    With a triumphant victory. Thou shalt visit him;
    We will to court, where if it be thy pleasure,
    Thou shalt appear in such a ravishing luster
    Of jewels above value, that the dames
    Who brave it there, in rage to be outshin'd,   80
    Shall hide them in their closets, and unseen
    Fret in their tears, whiles every wond'ring eye
    Shall crave none other brightness but thy presence.
    Choose thine own recreations. Be a queen
    Of what delights thou fanciest best, what company,   85
    What place, what times; do anything, do all things
    Youth can command, so thou wilt chase these clouds
    From the pure firmament of thy fair looks.

GRAUSIS.

    Now 'tis well said, my lord. —What, lady? Laugh,
    Be merry. Time is precious.

BASSANES [*aside*].   Furies whip thee!   90

PENTHEA.

    Alas my lord, this language to your handmaid

---

  65. *huddle*] crowd.

  80. *brave it*] display their finery.

  90. *Furies*] In Roman mythology the Furiae (patterned after the Greek
Erinyes, or Eumenides) were female divinities who punished evildoers.
In one hand they held a torch; in the other, a whip of scorpions.

Sounds as would music to the deaf. I need
No braveries nor cost of art to draw
The whiteness of my name into offense.
Let such, if any such there are, who covet   95
A curiosity of admiration,
By laying out their plenty to full view,
Appear in gaudy outsides; my attires
Shall suit the inward fashion of my mind,
From which, if your opinion nobly plac'd   100
Change not the livery your words bestow,
My fortunes with my hopes are at the highest.

BASSANES.

This house, methinks, stands somewhat too much inward;
It is too melancholy. We'll remove
Nearer the court. Or what thinks my Penthea   105
Of the delightful island we command?
Rule me as thou canst wish.

PENTHEA.   I am no mistress.
Whither you please, I must attend; all ways
Are alike pleasant to me.

GRAUSIS.   Island? Prison.
A prison is as gaysome. We'll no islands.   110
Marry, out upon 'em! Whom shall we see there?
Seagulls, and porpoises, and water rats,
And crabs, and mews, and dogfish; goodly gear
For a young lady's dealing, or an old one's.
On no terms islands; I'll be stew'd first.

BASSANES [*aside to* Grausis].   Grausis,   115
You are a juggling bawd. —This sadness, sweetest,
Becomes not youthful blood. —[*Aside to* Grausis.]
                                I'll have you pounded.—
For my sake put on a more cheerful mirth.
Thou't mar thy cheeks and make me old in griefs.—
[*Aside to* Grausis.]   Damnable bitch-fox!

GRAUSIS.   I am thick of hearing 120

---

103. *inward*] secluded.   104. *remove*] move.
113. *mews*] gulls.   116. *juggling*] cheating.
117. *pounded*] impounded.

Still when the wind blows southerly. What think 'ee
If your fresh lady breed young bones, my lord?
Would not a chopping boy d'ee good at heart?
But as you said—

BASSANES [*aside to* Grausis].   I'll spit thee on a stake,
Or chop thee into collops.

GRAUSIS.   Pray speak louder.   125
Sure, sure, the wind blows south still.

PENTHEA.   Thou prat'st madly.

BASSANES.

'Tis very hot; I sweat extremely. —Now?

Enter Phulas.

PHULAS.

A herd of lords, sir.

BASSANES.   Ha?

PHULAS.   A flock of ladies.

BASSANES.

Where?

PHULAS.   Shoals of horses.

BASSANES.   Peasant, how?

PHULAS.   Caroches
In drifts. Th'one enter, th'other stand without, sir.   130
And now I vanish.   *Exit* Phulas.

Enter Prophilus, *Hemophil, Groneas, Christalla, and Philema.*

PROPHILUS.   Noble Bassanes.

BASSANES.

Most welcome, Prophilus; ladies, gentlemen,
To all my heart is open; you all honor me—
[*Aside.*]   A tympany swells in my head already—
Honor me bountifully. —[*Aside.*]   How they flutter,   135

---

123. *chopping*] strapping.   125. *collops*] slices.
129. *Shoals*] flocks, schools (of fish).
129. *Caroches*] "the 17th c. name of a coach or chariot of a stately or
luxurious kind" (*OED*).
130. *drifts*] "a number of animals driven or moving along in a body; a
drove, herd, flock" (*OED*).
134. *tympany*] (1) a morbid swelling or tumor; (2) a distention, inflation.

Wagtails and jays together!

PROPHILUS. From your brother,
By virtue of your love to him, I require
Your instant presence, fairest.

PENTHEA. He is well, sir?

PROPHILUS.
The gods preserve him ever. Yet, dear beauty,
I find some alteration in him lately 140
Since his return to Sparta. —My good lord,
I pray use no delay.

BASSANES. We had not needed
An invitation if his sister's health
Had not fallen into question. —Haste, Penthea;
Slack not a minute. —Lead the way, good Prophilus; 145
I'll follow step by step.

PROPHILUS. Your arm, fair madam.

Exeunt omnes sed Bassanes *et* Grausis.

BASSANES.
One word with your old bawdship: th' hadst been better
Rail'd at the sins thou worshipp'st than have thwarted
My will. I'll use thee cursedly.

GRAUSIS. You dote,
You are beside yourself. A politician 150
In jealousy? No, y'are too gross, too vulgar.
Pish, teach not me my trade; I know my cue.
My crossing you sinks me into her trust,
By which I shall know all. My trade's a sure one.

BASSANES.
Forgive me, Grausis; 'twas consideration 155
I relish'd not. But have a care now.

GRAUSIS. Fear not,
I am no new-come-to't.

BASSANES. Thy life's upon it,
And so is mine. My agonies are infinite. *Exeunt omnes.*

---

136. *Wagtails*] "The name of these birds was often applied to wanton women" (Spencer).

136. *jays*] (1) impertinent chatterers; (2) flashy women, especially of light character.

146.1. *sed*] but.

[II.ii]   *Enter* Ithocles, *alone.*

ITHOCLES.

    Ambition? 'Tis of vipers' breed; it gnaws
    A passage through the womb that gave it motion.
    Ambition, like a seeled dove, mounts upward,
    Higher and higher still, to perch on clouds,
    But tumbles headlong down with heavier ruin.   5
    So squibs and crackers fly into the air;
    Then only breaking with a noise, they vanish
    In stench and smoke. Morality applied
    To timely practice keeps the soul in tune,
    At whose sweet music all our actions dance.   10
    But this is form of books and school tradition;
    It physics not the sickness of a mind
    Broken with griefs. Strong fevers are not eas'd
    With counsel, but with best receipts and means.
    Means, speedy means and certain; that's the cure.   15

Enter Armostes *and* Crotolon.

ARMOSTES.

    You stick, Lord Crotolon, upon a point
    Too nice and too unnecessary. Prophilus
    Is every way desertful. I am confident
    Your wisdom is too ripe to need instruction

1–2. *vipers' . . . motion*] an allusion to the belief that the female viper is killed by her young eating their way out of her womb. Cf. Pliny, X.lxxxii.

    3. *seeled*] with eyelids sewed together.

3–5. *dove . . . ruin*] The "sport" was to release and watch the blinded bird, which would soar straight up until exhausted, then fall to the earth. Cf. Sidney's sonnet in *The Complete Works of Sir Philip Sidney*, ed. A. Feuillerat (Cambridge, 1912–1926), II, 308: "Like as the dove, which seeled up, doth fly/ Is neither freed, nor yet to service bound;/ But hopes to get some help by mounting high,/ Till want of force do force her to the ground."

    6. *squibs*] "a common species of firework, in which the burning of the composition is usually terminated by a slight explosion" (*OED*). Cf. Ford's poem *Christes Bloodie Sweate* (1613), p. 34: "Yet as a cunning fire-work lighted glowes,/ Spits and with hissing wonders dares the skies,/ Till being wasted, downe it fal, and showes/ No more; his matter spent it weakely dies,/ And vanisheth to aire and smoke, so men/ In health are strong, but dying vanish then."

    17. *nice*] scrupulous, fine.

From your son's tutelage.

CROTOLON.   Yet not so ripe,   20
My Lord Armostes, that it dares to dote
Upon the painted meat of smooth persuasion
Which tempts me to a breach of faith.

ITHOCLES.   Not yet
Resolv'd, my lord? Why if your son's consent
Be so available, we'll write to Athens   25
For his repair to Sparta. The king's hand
Will join with our desires; he has been mov'd to't.

ARMOSTES.

Yes, and the king himself importun'd Crotolon
For a dispatch.

CROTOLON.   Kings may command; their wills
Are laws not to be questioned.

ITHOCLES.   By this marriage   30
You knit an union so devout, so hearty,
Between your loves to me, and mine to yours,
As if mine own blood had an interest in it;
For Prophilus is mine, and I am his.

CROTOLON.

My lord, my lord.

ITHOCLES.   What, good sir? Speak your thought.   35

CROTOLON.

Had this sincerity been real once,
My Orgilus had not been now unwiv'd,
Nor your lost sister buried in a bridebed.
Your uncle here, Armostes, knows this truth,
For had your father Thrasus liv'd—but peace   40
Dwell in his grave. I have done.

ARMOSTES.   Y'are bold and bitter.

ITHOCLES [*aside*].

'A presses home the injury, it smarts.—
No reprehensions, uncle; I deserve 'em.
Yet gentle sir, consider what the heat
Of an unsteady youth, a giddy brain,   45
Green indiscretion, flattery of greatness,

---

22. *painted*] counterfeit.
25. *available*] advantageous.

Rawness of judgment, willfulness in folly,
Thoughts vagrant as the wind and as uncertain,
Might lead a boy in years to. 'Twas a fault,
A capital fault, for then I could not dive 50
Into the secrets of commanding love;
Since when, experience by the extremities (in others)
Hath forc'd me to collect. And trust me, Crotolon,
I will redeem those wrongs with any service
Your satisfaction can require for current. 55

ARMOSTES.
Thy acknowledgment is satisfaction.—
What would you more?

CROTOLON.   I'm conquer'd. If Euphranea
Herself admit the motion, let it be so.
I doubt not my son's liking.

ITHOCLES.   Use my fortunes,
Life, power, sword, and heart; all are your own. 60

Enter Bassanes, Prophilus, Calantha, Penthea, Euphranea, *Christalla,
Philema, and Grausis.*

ARMOSTES.
The princess, with your sister.

CALANTHA.   I present 'ee
A stranger here in court, my lord, for did not
Desire of seeing you draw her abroad,
We had not been made happy in her company.

ITHOCLES.
You are a gracious princess. —Sister, wedlock 65
Holds too severe a passion in your nature,
Which can engross all duty to your husband
Without attendance on so dear a mistress.—
'Tis not my brother's pleasure, I presume,
T' immure her in a chamber.

BASSANES.   'Tis her will, 70
She governs her own hours. Noble Ithocles,
We thank the gods for your success and welfare.

64. We] *Q (corr.)*; She *Q (uncorr.)*.

---

53. *collect*] comprehend.
55. *current*] "a metaphor taken from coin that is current" (Weber).

    Our lady has of late been indispos'd,
    Else we had waited on you with the first.

ITHOCLES.

    How does Penthea now?

PENTHEA.   You best know, brother,   75
    From whom my health and comforts are deriv'd.

BASSANES [*aside*].

    I like the answer well; 'tis sad and modest.
    There may be tricks yet, tricks. —Have an eye, Grausis.

CALANTHA.

    Now Crotolon, the suit we join'd in must not
    Fall by too long demur.

CROTOLON.   'Tis granted, princess,   80
    For my part.

ARMOSTES.   With condition that his son
    Favor the contract.

CALANTHA.   Such delay is easy.—
    The joys of marriage make thee, Prophilus,
    A proud deserver of Euphranea's love,
    And her of thy desert.

PROPHILUS.   Most sweetly gracious.   85

BASSANES.

    The joys of marriage are the heaven on earth,
    Life's paradise, great princess, the soul's quiet,
    Sinews of concord, earthly immortality,
    Eternity of pleasures; no restoratives
    Like to a constant woman. —[*Aside.*]   But where is she?   90
    'Twould puzzle all the gods but to create
    Such a new monster. —I can speak by proof,
    For I rest in Elysium; 'tis my happiness.

CROTOLON.

    Euphranea, how are you resolv'd (speak freely)
    In your affections to this gentleman?   95

EUPHRANEA.

    Nor more nor less than as his love assures me,

---

    77. *sad*] sober, serious.   80. *demur*] delay.
    88. *Sinews of concord*] strength of love; also, possibly a pun in terms of music, *sinews* meaning "strings of an instrument" and *concord* "harmony" (opposite of "discord").

Which (if your liking with my brother's warrants)
I cannot but approve in all points worthy.

CROTOLON.

So, so. —[*To* Prophilus.]   I know your answer.

ITHOCLES.   'T had been pity
To sunder hearts so equally consented.   100

Enter Hemophil.

HEMOPHIL.

The king, Lord Ithocles, commands your presence;
And, fairest princess, yours.

CALANTHA.   We will attend him.

Enter Groneas.

GRONEAS.

Where are the lords? All must unto the king
Without delay. The Prince of Argos—

CALANTHA.   Well sir?

GRONEAS.

Is coming to the court, sweet lady.

CALANTHA.   How!   105
The Prince of Argos?

GRONEAS.   'Twas my fortune, madam,
T'enjoy the honor of these happy tidings.

ITHOCLES.

Penthea.

PENTHEA.   Brother?

ITHOCLES.   Let me an hour hence
Meet you alone within the palace grove;
I have some secret with you.—[*To* Prophilus.] Prithee friend, 110
Conduct her thither, and have special care
The walks be clear'd of any to disturb us.

PROPHILUS.

I shall.

BASSANES [*aside*].   How's that?

ITHOCLES.   Alone, pray be alone.—
I am your creature, princess. —On, my lords.

                              Exeunt [*all but*] Bassanes.

---

104. *Argos*] a state northeast of Laconia in Peloponnesus.

BASSANES.

> Alone, alone? What means that word "alone"?   115
> Why might not I be there? Hum! He's her brother;
> Brothers and sisters are but flesh and blood,
> And this same whoreson court-ease is temptation
> To a rebellion in the veins. Besides,
> His fine friend Prophilus must be her guardian.   120
> Why may not he dispatch a business nimbly
> Before the other come? Or pand'ring, pand'ring
> For one another (be't to sister, mother,
> Wife, cousin, anything) 'mongst youths of mettle
> Is in request. It is so; stubborn fate.   125
> But if I be a cuckold and can know it,
> I will be fell, and fell.

Enter Groneas.

GRONEAS.   My lord, y'are call'd for.

BASSANES.

> Most heartily I thank ye. Where's my wife, pray?

GRONEAS.

> Retir'd amongst the ladies.

BASSANES.   Still I thank 'ee.

> There's an old waiter with her; saw you her too?   130

GRONEAS.

> She sits i'th' presence lobby fast asleep, sir.

BASSANES.

> Asleep? Sleep, sir?

GRONEAS.   Is your lordship troubled?

> You will not to the king?

BASSANES.   Your humblest vassal.

GRONEAS.

> Your servant, my good lord.

BASSANES.   I wait your footsteps.   *Exeunt.*

[II.iii]   [*Enter*] Prophilus, Penthea.

PROPHILUS.

> In this walk, lady, will your brother find you.

---

127. *fell*] ruthless.   130. *waiter*] attendant.

And with your favor, give me leave a little
To work a preparation. In his fashion
I have observ'd of late some kind of slackness
To such alacrity as nature once   5
And custom took delight in. Sadness grows
Upon his recreations, which he hoards
In such a willing silence that to question
The grounds will argue little skill in friendship,
And less good manners.

PENTHEA.   Sir, I'm not inquisitive   10
Of secrecies without an invitation.

PROPHILUS.

With pardon, lady, not a syllable
Of mine implies so rude a sense; the drift—

            Enter Orgilus [, *disguised as before*].

Do thy best
To make this lady merry for an hour.   *Exit.*   15

ORGILUS.

Your will shall be a law, sir.

PENTHEA.   Prithee leave me,
I have some private thoughts I would account with.
Use thou thine own.

ORGILUS.   Speak on, fair nymph; our souls
Can dance as well to music of the spheres
As any's who have feasted with the gods.   20

PENTHEA.

Your school terms are too troublesome.

ORGILUS.   What heaven
Refines mortality from dross of earth
But such as uncompounded beauty hallows
With glorified perfection?

PENTHEA.   Set thy wits
In a less wild proportion.

ORGILUS.   Time can never   25
On the white table of unguilty faith

5. once] *Gifford; not in Q.*   9. little] *Weber; not in Q.*

23. *uncompounded*] "unmixed; not made up of various elements"; often
used to describe God or his essence (*OED*).
    26. *table*] tablet.

Write counterfeit dishonor. Turn those eyes,
The arrows of pure love, upon that fire
Which once rose to a flame, perfum'd with vows
As sweetly scented as the incense smoking   30
On Vesta's altars; virgin tears, like
The holiest odors, sprinkled dews to feed 'em
And to increase their fervor.

PENTHEA.   Be not frantic.

ORGILUS.

All pleasures are but mere imagination,
Feeding the hungry appetite with steam   35
And sight of banquet, whilst the body pines,
Not relishing the real taste of food.
Such is the leanness of a heart divided
From intercourse of troth-contracted loves;
No horror should deface that precious figure   40
Seal'd with the lively stamp of equal souls.

PENTHEA.

Away! Some fury hath bewitch'd thy tongue.
The breath of ignorance that flies from thence,
Ripens a knowledge in me of afflictions
Above all suff'rance. Thing of talk, be gone;   45
Be gone without reply.

ORGILUS.   Be just, Penthea,
In thy commands. When thou send'st forth a doom
Of banishment, know first on whom it lights.
Thus I take off the shroud in which my cares
Are folded up from view of common eyes.   50

                    [*Throws off his scholar's gown.*]

What is thy sentence next?

PENTHEA.   Rash man, thou layest
A blemish on mine honor with the hazard
Of thy too desperate life. Yet I profess,
By all the laws of ceremonious wedlock,
I have not given admittance to one thought   55
Of female change since cruelty enforc'd

31–32. On Vesta's . . . / The holiest]   Vesta's *Q*.
Oliphant; The holiest . . ./ On   31. altars] *Weber;* Artars *Q*.

−40−

Divorce betwixt my body and my heart.
Why would you fall from goodness thus?

ORGILUS.   O, rather
Examine me how I could live to say
I have been much, much wrong'd. 'Tis for thy sake   60
I put on this imposture. Dear Penthea,
If thy soft bosom be not turn'd to marble,
Thou't pity our calamities; my interest
Confirms me thou art mine still.

PENTHEA.   Lend your hand;
With both of mine I clasp it thus, thus kiss it,   65
Thus kneel before ye.

ORGILUS.   You instruct my duty.

PENTHEA.
We may stand up. Have you aught else to urge
Of new demand? As for the old, forget it;
'Tis buried in an everlasting silence,
And shall be, shall be ever. What more would ye?   70

ORGILUS.
I would possess my wife; the equity
Of very reason bids me.

PENTHEA.   Is that all?

ORGILUS.
Why 'tis the all of me, myself.

PENTHEA.   Remove
Your steps some distance from me; at this space
A few words I dare change. But first put on   75
Your borrowed shape.

ORGILUS.   You are obey'd, 'tis done.

PENTHEA.
How, Orgilus, by promise I was thine,
The heavens do witness; they can witness too
A rape done on my truth. How I do love thee
Yet, Orgilus, and yet, must best appear   80
In tendering thy freedom, for I find
The constant preservation of thy merit

67. aught] ought Q.

---

75. *change*] exchange.
76. *borrowed shape*] disguise.

By thy not daring to attempt my fame
With injury of any loose conceit,
Which might give deeper wounds to discontents.　　　85
Continue this fair race; then though I cannot
Add to thy comfort, yet I shall more often
Remember from what fortune I am fallen,
And pity mine own ruin. Live, live happy,
Happy in thy next choice, that thou mayst people　　90
This barren age with virtues in thy issue.
And O, when thou art married, think on me
With mercy, not contempt. I hope thy wife,
Hearing my story, will not scorn my fall.
Now let us part.

ORGILUS.　　　　　　Part! Yet advise thee better:　　95
Penthea is the wife to Orgilus,
And ever shall be.

PENTHEA.　　　　　　Never shall nor will.

ORGILUS.
How!

PENTHEA.　　Hear me; in a word I'll tell thee why.
The virgin dowry which my birth bestow'd
Is ravish'd by another. My true love　　　　　　100
Abhors to think that Orgilus deserv'd
No better favors than a second bed.

ORGILUS.
I must not take this reason.

PENTHEA.　　　　　　　To confirm it,
Should I outlive my bondage, let me meet
Another worse than this and less desir'd,　　　　105
If of all the men alive thou shouldst but touch
My lip or hand again.

ORGILUS.　　　　　　Penthea, now
I tell 'ee you grow wanton in my sufferance;
Come sweet, th'art mine.

PENTHEA.　　　　　　Uncivil sir, forbear,
Or I can turn affection into vengeance.　　　　110
Your reputation, if you value any,

---

83. *attempt my fame*] i.e., attack my reputation.
108. *wanton*] reckless.

Lies bleeding at my feet. Unworthy man,
If ever henceforth thou appear in language,
Message, or letter to betray my frailty,
I'll call thy former protestations lust, 115
And curse my stars for forfeit of my judgment.
Go thou, fit only for disguise and walks,
To hide thy shame. This once I spare thy life.
I laugh at mine own confidence; my sorrows
By thee are made inferior to my fortunes. 120
If ever thou didst harbor worthy love,
Dare not to answer. My good genius guide me,
That I may never see thee more. Go from me.

ORGILUS.

I'll tear my veil of politic French off,
And stand up like a man resolv'd to do. 125
Action, not words, shall show me. O, Penthea! *Exit* Orgilus.

PENTHEA.

'A sigh'd my name sure as he parted from me;
I fear I was too rough. Alas poor gentleman,
'A look'd not like the ruins of his youth,
But like the ruins of those ruins. Honor, 130
How much we fight with weakness to preserve thee.

Enter Bassanes *and* Grausis.

BASSANES.

Fie on thee! Damn thee, rotten maggot, damn thee!
Sleep? Sleep at court? And now? Aches, convulsions,
Impostumes, rheums, gouts, palsies clog thy bones
A dozen years more yet.

GRAUSIS.   Now y'are in humors. 135

BASSANES.

She's by herself; there's hope of that. She's sad too;

124. I'll] *Gifford;* I'e *Q.*   134. rheums] *Weber;* rhemes *Q.*

---

124. *tear . . . off*] i.e., abandon my disguise. Here *French*—an obvious
anachronism in ancient Sparta—connotes dissimulation; cf. Ford's *Perkin
Warbeck:* "Yet this was all but French dissimulation,/ Aiming at peace with
us" (I.i.112–113); and his *Love's Sacrifice:* "The French are passing courtly,
ripe of wit,/ Kind, but extreme dissemblers" (I.i.131–132).
133. *Aches*] here a dissyllable, pronounced "aitches."
134. *Impostumes*] abscesses.

She's in strong contemplation. Yes, and fix'd.
The signs are wholesome.

GRAUSIS.   Very wholesome, truly.

BASSANES.

Hold your chops, nightmare. —Lady, come. Your brother
Is carried to his closet; you must thither.   140

PENTHEA.

Not well, my lord?

BASSANES.   A sudden fit, 'twill off;
Some surfeit or disorder. How dost, dearest?

PENTHEA.

Your news is none o'th' best.

Enter Prophilus.

PROPHILUS.   The chief of men,
The excellentest Ithocles, desires
Your presence, madam.

BASSANES.   We are hasting to him.   145

PENTHEA.

In vain we labor in this course of life
To piece our journey out at length, or crave
Respite of breath. Our home is in the grave.

BASSANES.

Perfect philosophy. Then let us care
To live so that our reckonings may fall even   150
When w'are to make account.

PROPHILUS.   He cannot fear
Who builds on noble grounds. Sickness or pain
Is the deserver's exercise, and such
Your virtuous brother to the world is known.
Speak comfort to him, lady; be all gentle.   155
Stars fall but in the grossness of our sight;
A good man dying, th'earth doth lose a light.   *Exeunt omnes.*

---

139. *chops*] jaws.
150. *fall even*] "having no balance or debt on either side" (*OED*).
153. *exercise*] discipline.

[III.i]   *Enter* Tecnicus, *and* Orgilus *in his own shape.*

TECNICUS.

    Be well advised; let not a resolution

    Of giddy rashness choke the breath of reason.

ORGILUS.

    It shall not, most sage master.

TECNICUS.   I am jealous.

    For if the borrowed shape so late put on

    Inferr'd a consequence, we must conclude   5

    Some violent design of sudden nature

    Hath shook that shadow off, to fly upon

    A new-hatch'd execution. Orgilus,

    Take heed thou hast not, under our integrity,

    Shrouded unlawful plots. Our mortal eyes   10

    Pierce not the secrets of your hearts; the gods

    Are only privy to them.

ORGILUS.   Learned Tecnicus,

    Such doubts are causeless, and to clear the truth

    From misconceit, the present state commands me.

    The Prince of Argos comes himself in person   15

    In quest of great Calantha for his bride,

    Our kingdom's heir; besides, mine only sister,

    Euphranea, is dispos'd to Prophilus.

    Lastly, the king is sending letters for me

    To Athens, for my quick repair to court.   20

    Please to accept these reasons.

TECNICUS.   Just ones, Orgilus,

    Not to be contradicted. Yet beware

    Of an unsure foundation; no fair colors

    Can fortify a building faintly jointed.

    I have observ'd a growth in thy aspect   25

    Of dangerous extent, sudden, and (look to 't)

    I might add, certain—

ORGILUS.   My aspect? Could art

    Run through mine inmost thoughts, it should not sift

---

   3. *jealous*] suspicious.

   7. *shadow*] disguise.

  14. *misconceit*] misconception.

An inclination there more than what suited
With justice of mine honor.

TECNICUS.   I believe it.   30
But know then, Orgilus, what honor is:
Honor consists not in a bare opinion
By doing any act that feeds content,
Brave in appearance 'cause we think it brave.
Such honor comes by accident, not nature,   35
Proceeding from the vices of our passion,
Which makes our reason drunk. But real honor
Is the reward of virtue, and acquir'd
By justice or by valor, which for bases
Hath justice to uphold it. He then fails   40
In honor who for lucre or revenge
Commits thefts, murders, treasons, and adulteries,
With suchlike, by intrenching on just laws,
Whose sov'reignty is best preserv'd by justice.
Thus as you see how honor must be grounded   45
On knowledge, not opinion (for opinion
Relies on probability and accident,
But knowledge on necessity and truth),
I leave thee to the fit consideration
Of what becomes the grace of real honor,   50
Wishing success to all thy virtuous meanings.

ORGILUS.
The gods increase thy wisdom, reverend oracle,
And in thy precepts make me ever thrifty.

TECNICUS.
I thank thy wish.—   *Exit* Orgilus.
                Much mystery of fate
Lies hid in that man's fortunes; curiosity   55
May lead his actions into rare attempts.
But let the gods be moderators still,
No human power can prevent their will.—

Enter Armostes.

From whence come 'ee?

41. or] *Gifford;* of *Q*.   54. S.D.] *Gifford; after* thrifty (*l. 53*)
                                           Q.

ARMOSTES.   From King Amyclas; pardon
    My interruption of your studies. Here   60
    In this seal'd box he sends a treasure dear
    To him as his crown. 'A prays your gravity
    You would examine, ponder, sift, and bolt
    The pith and circumstance of every tittle
    The scroll within contains.
TECNICUS.   What is 't, Armostes?   65
ARMOSTES.
    It is the health of Sparta, the king's life,
    Sinews and safety of the commonwealth:
    The sum of what the oracle deliver'd
    When last he visited the prophetic temple
    At Delphos. What his reasons are for which,   70
    After so long a silence, he requires
    Your counsel now, grave man, his majesty
    Will soon himself acquaint you with.
TECNICUS.   Apollo
    Inspire my intellect! —The Prince of Argos
    Is entertain'd?
ARMOSTES.   He is, and has demanded   75
    Our princess for his wife, which I conceive
    One special cause the king importunes you
    For resolution of the oracle.
TECNICUS.
    My duty to the king, good peace to Sparta,
    And fair day to Armostes.
ARMOSTES.   Like to Tecnicus!   *Exeunt.*   80

[III.ii]   *Soft music. A song.*

                    Can you paint a thought, or number
                    Every fancy in a slumber?
                    Can you count soft minutes roving
                    From a dial's point by moving?

72. Your] *Weber;* You *Q.*

---

63. *bolt*] sift (literally, by means of a bolting-cloth).
75. *entertain'd*] received, welcomed.
78. *resolution*] interpretation.

> *Can you grasp a sigh or, lastly,*   5
> *Rob a virgin's honor chastely?*
> > *No, O, no. Yet you may*
> > > *Sooner do both that and this,*
> > > *This and that, and never miss,*
> > *Than by any praise display*   10
> > > *Beauty's beauty; such a glory*
> > > *As beyond all fate, all story,*
> > > > *All arms, all arts,*
> > > > *All loves, all hearts,*
> > *Greater than those or they,*   15
> > *Do, shall, and must obey.*

During which time, enters Prophilus, Bassanes, Penthea, Grausis, *passing over the stage;* Bassanes *and* Grausis *enter again softly, stealing to several stands, and listen.*

BASSANES.

    All silent, calm, secure. —Grausis, no creaking?
    No noise? Dost hear nothing?

GRAUSIS.   Not a mouse,
    Or whisper of the wind.

BASSANES.   The floor is matted,
    The bedposts sure are steel or marble. Soldiers   20
    Should not affect, methinks, strains so effeminate;
    Sounds of such delicacy are but fawnings
    Upon the sloth of luxury. They heighten
    Cinders of covert lust up to a flame.

GRAUSIS.

    What do you mean, my lord? Speak low; that gabbling   25
    Of yours will but undo us.

BASSANES.   Chamber combats
    Are felt, not heard.

PROPHILUS [*within*].   'A wakes.

BASSANES.   What's that?

27. heard] *Weber;* hard *Q.*

16.2–3. *several stands*] different positions.

19. *matted*] covered with mats, which were "pieces of coarse fabric formed by plaiting rushes, sedge, straw, bast, etc." (*OED*).

23. *luxury*] lust.

ITHOCLES [*within*].   Who's there?
   Sister? —All quit the room else.
BASSANES.   'Tis consented.

Enter Prophilus.

PROPHILUS.
   Lord Bassanes, your brother would be private;
   We must forbear. His sleep hath newly left him.   30
   Please 'ee withdraw.
BASSANES.   By any means; 'tis fit.
PROPHILUS.
   Pray gentlewoman, walk too.
GRAUSIS.   Yes, I will sir.   *Exeunt omnes.*

   Ithocles *discovered in a chair, and* Penthea.

ITHOCLES.
   Sit nearer, sister, to me; nearer yet.
   We had one father, in one womb took life,
   Were brought up twins together, yet have liv'd   35
   At distance like two strangers. I could wish
   That the first pillow whereon I was cradled
   Had prov'd to me a grave.
PENTHEA.   You had been happy.
   Then had you never known that sin of life
   Which blots all following glories with a vegeance   40
   For forfeiting the last will of the dead,
   From whom you had your being.
ITHOCLES.   Sad Penthea,
   Thou canst not be too cruel; my rash spleen
   Hath with a violent hand pluck'd from thy bosom
   A lover-bless'd heart to grind it into dust,   45
   For which mine's now a-breaking.
PENTHEA.   Not yet, heaven,
   I do beseech thee! First let some wild fires
   Scorch, not consume it. May the heat be cherish'd
   With desires infinite but hopes impossible.
ITHOCLES.
   Wrong'd soul, thy prayers are heard.
PENTHEA.   Here, lo, I breathe,   50
   A miserable creature led to ruin

By an unnatural brother.

ITHOCLES.   I consume
In languishing affections for that trespass,
Yet cannot die.

PENTHEA.   The handmaid to the wages
Of country toil drinks the untroubled streams   55
With leaping kids and with the bleating lambs,
And so allays her thirst secure, whiles I
Quench my hot sighs with fleetings of my tears.

ITHOCLES.

The laborer doth eat his coarsest bread,
Earn'd with his sweat, and lies him down to sleep,   60
While every bit I touch turns in digestion
To gall, as bitter as Penthea's curse.
Put me to any penance for my tyranny,
And I will call thee merciful.

PENTHEA.   Pray kill me,
Rid me from living with a jealous husband.   65
Then we will join in friendship, be again
Brother and sister. Kill me, pray. Nay, will 'ee?

ITHOCLES.

How does thy lord esteem thee?

PENTHEA.   Such an one
As only you have made me: a faith-breaker,
A spotted whore. Forgive me. I am one   70
In art, not in desires, the gods must witness.

ITHOCLES.

Thou dost belie thy friend.

PENTHEA.   I do not, Ithocles;
For she that's wife to Orgilus and lives
In known adultery with Bassanes
Is at the best a whore. Wilt kill me now?   75
The ashes of our parents will assume
Some dreadful figure and appear to charge

---

55. Of ... streams] *Gifford;* The   streames *Q.*
vntroubled of Country toyle, drinkes   61. While] *Gifford;* Which *Q.*

---

53. *affections*] emotions.
58. *fleetings*] (1) flowings; (2) skimmings, curds.
71. *art*] practice (?). Some editors emend to *act.*

Thy bloody guilt, that hast betray'd their name
To infamy in this reproachful match.

ITHOCLES.

    After my victories abroad, at home   80
I meet despair; ingratitude of nature
Hath made my actions monstrous. Thou shalt stand
A deity, my sister, and be worshipp'd
For thy resolved martyrdom. Wrong'd maids
And married wives shall to thy hallowed shrine   85
Offer their orisons, and sacrifice
Pure turtles crown'd with myrtle, if thy pity
Unto a yielding brother's pressure lend
One finger but to ease it.

PENTHEA.   O, no more!

ITHOCLES.

    Death waits to waft me to the Stygian banks   90
And free me from this chaos of my bondage.
And till thou wilt forgive, I must endure.

PENTHEA.

    Who is the saint you serve?

ITHOCLES.   Friendship, or nearness
Of birth to any but my sister, durst not
Have mov'd that question as a secret, sister,   95
I dare not murmur to myself.

PENTHEA.   Let me,
By your new protestations I conjure 'ee,
Partake her name.

ITHOCLES.   Her name—'tis—'tis—I dare not.

PENTHEA.

    All your respects are forg'd.

ITHOCLES.   They are not. —Peace.
Calantha is the princess, the king's daughter,   100

93. nearness] *Weber; not in Q.*

---

87. *turtles*] turtle-doves; "the emblem of faithful love" (Scollard).
88. *yielding*] succumbing, collapsing.
90. *Stygian*] pertaining to the Styx, principal river (according to Greek mythology) of the underworld; it had to be crossed in going to the land of the dead.
99. *All ... forg'd*] "All the considerations you have mentioned are feigned; i.e., your new attitude toward me is not genuine" (Spencer).

Sole heir of Sparta. —Me most miserable,
Do I now love thee? For my injuries
Revenge thyself with bravery, and gossip
My treasons to the king's ears; do. Calantha
Knows it not yet, nor Prophilus my nearest.   105

PENTHEA.

Suppose you were contracted to her, would it not
Split even your very soul to see her father
Snatch her out of your arms against her will,
And force her on the Prince of Argos?

ITHOCLES.   Trouble not
The fountains of mine eyes with thine own story.   110
I sweat in blood for't.

PENTHEA.   We are reconcil'd.
Alas sir, being children, but two branches
Of one stock, 'tis not fit we should divide.
Have comfort, you may find it.

ITHOCLES.   Yes, in thee.
Only in thee, Penthea mine.

PENTHEA.   If sorrows   115
Have not too much dull'd my infected brain,
I'll cheer invention for an active strain.

ITHOCLES.

Mad man! Why have I wrong'd a maid so excellent?

Enter Bassanes *with a poniard;* Prophilus, Groneas, Hemophil, *and* Grausis.

BASSANES.

I can forbear no longer. More, I will not.
Keep off your hands or fall upon my point.   120
Patience is tir'd, for like a slow-pac'd ass
Ye ride my easy nature, and proclaim
My sloth to vengeance a reproach and property.

ITHOCLES.

The meaning of this rudeness?

---

104. *treasons*] "For a subject to aspire to the hand of the heir to the throne might be construed as treasonable" (Sherman).
117. *I'll . . . strain*] "i.e., I will try to contrive some plan" (*BHN*).
123. *property*] characteristic.

PROPHILUS.   He's distracted.

PENTHEA.

    O, my griev'd lord!

GRAUSIS.   Sweet lady, come not near him;   125

    He holds his perilous weapon in his hand

    To prick 'a cares not whom nor where. —See, see, see!

BASSANES.

    My birth is noble, though the popular blast

    Of vanity, as giddy as thy youth,

    Hath rear'd thy name up to bestride a cloud   130

    Or progress in the chariot of the sun.

    I am no clod of trade to lackey pride,

    Nor like your slave of expectation wait

    The bawdy hinges of your doors, or whistle

    For mystical conveyance to your bed sports.   135

GRONEAS.

    Fine humors! They become him.

HEMOPHIL.   How 'a stares,

    Struts, puffs, and sweats. Most admirable lunacy!

ITHOCLES.

    But that I may conceive the spirit of wine

    Has took possession of your soberer custom,

    I'd say you were unmannerly.

PENTHEA.   Dear brother—   140

BASSANES.

    Unmannerly! Mew, kitling. Smooth formality

    Is usher to the rankness of the blood,

    But impudence bears up the train. Indeed, sir,

    Your fiery mettle, or your springal blaze

    Of huge renown, is no sufficient royalty   145

    To print upon my forehead the scorn "cuckold."

ITHOCLES.

    His jealousy has robb'd him of his wits;

    130–131. *bestride . . . sun*] references to Ixion and Phaeton, respectively;
cf. IV.i.69–71 and IV.iv.26.

    132. *lackey*] to wait upon as a lackey.

    137. *admirable*] remarkable.

    141. *kitling*] kitten.

    144. *springal*] youthful (cf. II.i.12, note).

    145. *royalty*] authority, warrant.

'A talks 'a knows not what.

BASSANES.   Yes, and 'a knows
To whom 'a talks: to one that franks his lust
In swine-security of bestial incest.   150

ITHOCLES.

Ha, devil!

BASSANES.   I will hallo 't, though I blush more
To name the filthiness than thou to act it.

ITHOCLES.

Monster!

PROPHILUS.   Sir, by our friendship—

PENTHEA.   By our bloods—
Will you quite both undo us, brother?

GRAUSIS.   Out on him.
These are his megrims, firks, and melancholies.   155

HEMOPHIL.

Well said, old touchhole.

GRONEAS.   Kick him out at doors.

PENTHEA.

With favor, let me speak. —My lord, what slackness
In my obedience hath deserv'd this rage?
Except humility and silent duty
Have drawn on your unquiet, my simplicity   160
Ne'er studied your vexation.

BASSANES.   Light of beauty,
Deal not ungently with a desperate wound.
No breach of reason dares make war with her
Whose looks are sovereignty, whose breath is balm.
O, that I could preserve thee in fruition   165
As in devotion.

PENTHEA.   Sir, may every evil
Lock'd in Pandora's box show'r, in your presence,
On my unhappy head, if since you made me

159. silent] *Weber;* sinlent *Q.*

149–150. *franks . . . security*] "small enclosures (*franks,* as distinguished
from styes) in which boars were fattened. As these animals were dangerous
when full-fed, it was necessary to shut them up alone . . . . the extreme of
grossness and sensuality is conveyed by the words *franked up*" (Gifford).
    151. *hallo*] proclaim.   155. *megrims*] whims.
    155. *firks*] caprices.

A partner in your bed, I have been faulty
In one unseemly thought against your honor.   170
ITHOCLES.
Purge not his griefs, Penthea.
BASSANES.   Yes, say on,
Excellent creature. —Good, be not a hindrance
To peace and praise of virtue. —O, my senses
Are charm'd with sounds celestial. —On, dear, on;
I never gave you one ill word; say, did I?   175
Indeed I did not.
PENTHEA.   Nor, by Juno's forehead,
Was I e'er guilty of a wanton error.
BASSANES.
A goddess; let me kneel.
GRAUSIS.   Alas, kind animal.
ITHOCLES.
No, but for penance.
BASSANES.   Noble sir, what is it?
With gladness I embrace it; yet pray let not   180
My rashness teach you to be too unmerciful.
ITHOCLES.
When you shall show good proof that manly wisdom,
Not oversway'd by passion or opinion,
Knows how to lead your judgment, then this lady,
Your wife, my sister, shall return in safety   185
Home to be guided by you. But till first
I can out of clear evidence approve it,
She shall be my care.
BASSANES.   Rip my bosom up,
I'll stand the execution with a constancy.
This torture is unsufferable.
ITHOCLES.   Well sir,   190
I dare not trust her to your fury.
BASSANES.   But
Penthea says not so.

184. your] *Weber; not in Q.*

---

176. *by Juno's*] appropriate here, since Juno, as symbol of the Roman
matron, presided over marriage and punished incontinence or lewdness in
wives.

PENTHEA.   She needs no tongue
　　To plead excuse who never purpos'd wrong.
HEMOPHIL [*to* Grausis].
　　Virgin of reverence and antiquity,
　　Stay you behind.
GRONEAS [*to* Grausis].   The court wants not your diligence.   195
　　　　　　　　　　　　　　Exeunt omnes, sed Bassanes *&* Grausis.
GRAUSIS.
　　What will you do, my lord? My lady's gone,
　　I am denied to follow.
BASSANES.   I may see her
　　Or speak to her once more?
GRAUSIS.   And feel her too, man.
　　Be of good cheer, she's your own flesh and bone.
BASSANES.
　　Diseases desperate must find cures alike.   200
　　She swore she has been true.
GRAUSIS.   True, on my modesty.
BASSANES.
　　Let him want truth who credits not her vows.
　　Much wrong I did her, but her brother infinite;
　　Rumor will voice me the contempt of manhood,
　　Should I run on thus. Some way I must try   205
　　To outdo art and cry a jealousy.   *Exeunt omnes.*

[III.iii]
Flourish. Enter Amyclas, Nearchus *leading* Calantha, Armostes, Crotolon, *Euphranea, Christalla, Philema, and Amelus.*

AMYCLAS.
　　Cousin of Argos, what the heavens have pleas'd
　　In their unchanging counsels to conclude
　　For both our kingdoms' weal, we must submit to.
　　Nor can we be unthankful to their bounties,
　　Who when we were even creeping to our grave,   5

5. grave] *Dyce;* graves *Q.*

200. *Diseases . . . alike*] proverbial; cf. Tilley, D 357.
206. *art*] skill.
206. *cry a*] exclaim against.

Sent us a daughter, in whose birth our hope
Continues of succession. As you are
In title next, being grandchild to our aunt,
So we in heart desire you may sit nearest
Calantha's love, since we have ever vow'd   10
Not to enforce affection by our will,
But by her own choice to confirm it gladly.

NEARCHUS.

You speak the nature of a right just father.
I come not hither roughly to demand
My cousin's thralldom, but to free mine own.   15
Report of great Calantha's beauty, virtue,
Sweetness, and singular perfections courted
All ears to credit what I find was publish'd
By constant truth, from which if any service
Of my desert can purchase fair construction,   20
This lady must command it.

CALANTHA.   Princely sir,
So well you know how to profess observance
That you instruct your hearers to become
Practitioners in duty, of which number
I'll study to be chief.

NEARCHUS.   Chief, glorious virgin,   25
In my devotions, as in all men's wonder.

AMYCLAS.

Excellent cousin, we deny no liberty;
Use thine own opportunities. —Armostes,
We must consult with the philosophers.
The business is of weight.

ARMOSTES.   Sir, at your pleasure.   30

AMYCLAS.

You told me, Crotolon, your son's return'd
From Athens? Wherefore comes 'a not to court
As we commanded?

CROTOLON.   He shall soon attend
Your royal will, great sir.

AMYCLAS.   The marriage
Between young Prophilus and Euphranea   35

_____

22. *observance*] courtship.

Tastes of too much delay.

CROTOLON.   My lord.

AMYCLAS.   Some pleasures
At celebration of it would give life
To th'entertainment of the prince our kinsman.
Our court wears gravity more than we relish.

ARMOSTES.

Yet the heavens smile on all your high attempts   40
Without a cloud.

CROTOLON.   So may the gods protect us.

CALANTHA.

A prince a subject?

NEARCHUS.   Yes, to beauty's scepter.
As all hearts kneel, so mine.

CALANTHA.   You are too courtly.

[*Enter*] *to them*, Ithocles, Orgilus, Prophilus.

ITHOCLES.

Your safe return to Sparta is most welcome.
I joy to meet you here, and as occasion   45
Shall grant us privacy, will yield you reasons
Why I should covet to deserve the title
Of your respected friend. For without compliment
Believe it, Orgilus, 'tis my ambition.

ORGILUS.

Your lordship may command me your poor servant.   50

ITHOCLES [*aside*].

So amorously close? So soon? My heart!

PROPHILUS.

What sudden change is next?

ITHOCLES.   Life to the king,
To whom I here present this noble gentleman,
New come from Athens. Royal sir, vouchsafe
Your gracious hand in favor of his merit.   55

CROTOLON [*aside*].

My son preferr'd by Ithocles!

---

51. close] *Dyce;* close close *Q.*

56. *preferr'd*] put forward.

AMYCLAS.   Our bounties
    Shall open to thee, Orgilus. For instance,
    Hark in thine ear; if out of those inventions
    Which flow in Athens, thou hast there engross'd
    Some rarity of wit to grace the nuptials   60
    Of thy fair sister, and renown our court
    In th'eyes of this young prince, we shall be debtor
    To thy conceit. Think on 't.
ORGILUS.   Your highness honors me.
NEARCHUS.
    My tongue and heart are twins.
CALANTHA.   A noble birth,
    Becoming such a father. —Worthy Orgilus,   65
    You are a guest most wish'd for.
ORGILUS.   May my duty
    Still rise in your opinion, sacred princess.
ITHOCLES.
    Euphranea's brother, sir; a gentleman
    Well worthy of your knowledge.
NEARCHUS.   We embrace him,
    Proud of so dear acquaintance.
AMYCLAS.   All prepare   70
    For revels and disport. The joys of Hymen,
    Like Phoebus in his luster, puts to flight
    All mists of dullness. Crown the hours with gladness.
    No sounds but music, no discourse but mirth.
CALANTHA.
    Thine arm I prithee, Ithocles. —Nay, good   75
    My lord, keep on your way, I am provided.
NEARCHUS.
    I dare not disobey.
ITHOCLES.   Most heavenly lady.   *Exeunt.*

[III.iv]   *Enter* Crotolon, Orgilus.

CROTOLON.
    The king hath spoke his mind.
ORGILUS.   His will he hath,

---

59. *engross'd*] acquired.   71. *disport*] entertainment.

But were it lawful to hold plea against
The power of greatness, not the reason, haply
Such undershrubs as subjects sometimes might
Borrow of nature justice, to inform   5
That license sovereignty holds without check
Over a meek obedience.

CROTOLON.   How resolve you
Touching your sister's marriage? Prophilus
Is a deserving and a hopeful youth.

ORGILUS.
I envy not his merit but applaud it,   10
Could wish him thrift in all his best desires,
And with a willingness inleague our blood
With his for purchase of full growth in friendship.
He never touch'd on any wrong that malic'd
The honor of our house, nor stirr'd our peace;   15
Yet, with your favor, let me not forget
Under whose wing he gathers warmth and comfort,
Whose creature he is bound, made, and must live so.

CROTOLON.
Son, son, I find in thee a harsh condition.
No courtesy can win it; 'tis too rancorous.   20

ORGILUS.
Good sir, be not severe in your construction.
I am no stranger to such easy calms
As sit in tender bosoms. Lordly Ithocles
Hath grac'd my entertainment in abundance,
Too humbly hath descended from that height   25
Of arrogance and spleen which wrought the rape
On griev'd Penthea's purity; his scorn
Of my untoward fortunes is reclaim'd
Unto a courtship, almost to a fawning.
I'll kiss his foot, since you will have it so.   30

CROTOLON.
Since I will have it so? Friend, I will have it so,
Without our ruin by your politic plots

11. wish] *Weber;* with *Q.*

5–6. *inform . . . license*] i.e., direct, or guide, that authority.
11. *thrift*] success.
14. *malic'd*] sought to harm.   19. *condition*] disposition.

Or wolf of hatred snarling in your breast.
You have a spirit, sir, have ye? a familiar
That posts i'th' air for your intelligence?   35
Some such hobgoblin hurried you from Athens,
For yet you come unsent for.

ORGILUS.   If unwelcome,
I might have found a grave there.

CROTOLON.   Sure your business
Was soon dispatch'd, or your mind alter'd quickly.

ORGILUS.
'Twas care, sir, of my health cut short my journey;   40
For there a general infection
Threatens a desolation.

CROTOLON.   And I fear
Thou hast brought back a worse infection with thee:
Infection of thy mind, which, as thou say'st,
Threatens the desolation of our family.   45

ORGILUS.
Forbid it, our dear genius! I will rather
Be made a sacrifice on Thrasus' monument,
Or kneel to Ithocles his son in dust,
Than woo a father's curse. My sister's marriage
With Prophilus is from my heart confirm'd.   50
May I live hated, may I die despis'd,
If I omit to further it in all
That can concern me.

CROTOLON.   I have been too rough.
My duty to my king made me so earnest;
Excuse it, Orgilus.

ORGILUS.   Dear sir.

Enter to them, Prophilus, Euphranea, Ithocles, Groneas, Hemophil.

CROTOLON.   Here comes   55
Euphranea, with Prophilus and Ithocles.

ORGILUS.
Most honored, ever famous.

ITHOCLES.   Your true friend,
On earth not any truer. With smooth eyes
Look on this worthy couple; your consent

---

58. *smooth*] friendly.

Can only make them one.

ORGILUS.   They have it. —Sister,   60
    Thou pawn'dst to me an oath, of which engagement
    I never will release thee if thou aim'st
    At any other choice than this.

EUPHRANEA.   Dear brother,
    At him or none.

CROTOLON.   To which my blessing's added.

ORGILUS.
    Which till a greater ceremony perfect—   65
    Euphranea, lend thy hand. —Here, take her, Prophilus.
    Live long a happy man and wife; and further,
    That these in presence may conclude an omen,
    Thus for a bridal song I close my wishes:

> *Comforts lasting, loves increasing,*   70
> *Like soft hours never ceasing;*
> *Plenty's pleasure, peace complying*
> *Without jars or tongues envying;*
> *Hearts by holy union wedded*
> *More than theirs by custom bedded;*   75
> *Fruitful issues; life so graced*
> *Not by age to be defaced,*
> *Budding, as the year ensu'th,*
> *Every spring another youth:*
> *All what thought can add beside*   80
> *Crown this bridegroom and this bride.*

PROPHILUS.
    You have seal'd joy close to my soul. —Euphranea,
    Now I may call thee mine.

ITHOCLES.   I but exchange
    One good friend for another.

ORGILUS.   If these gallants
    Will please to grace a poor invention   85
    By joining with me in some slight device,
    I'll venture on a strain my younger days
    Have studied for delight.

HEMOPHIL.   With thankful willingness
    I offer my attendance.

---

61. *pawn'dst*] pledged.

GRONEAS.   No endeavor
    Of mine shall fail to show itself.

ITHOCLES.   We will   90
    All join to wait on thy directions, Orgilus.

ORGILUS.
    O, my good lord, your favors flow towards
    A too unworthy worm. But as you please;
    I am what you will shape me.

ITHOCLES.   A fast friend.

CROTOLON.
    I thank thee, son, for this acknowledgement.   95
    It is a sight of gladness.

ORGILUS.   But my duty.   *Exeunt omnes.*

[III.v]   *Enter* Calantha, Penthea, Christalla, Philema.

CALANTHA.
    Whoe'er would speak with us, deny his entrance;
    Be careful of our charge.

CHRISTALLA.   We shall, madam.

CALANTHA.
    Except the king himself, give none admittance,
    Not any.

PHILEMA.   Madam, it shall be our care.
                  Exeunt [Christalla *and* Philema].

CALANTHA.
    Being alone, Penthea, you have granted   5
    The opportunity you sought, and might
    At all times have commanded.

PENTHEA.   'Tis a benefit
    Which I shall owe your goodness even in death for.
    My glass of life, sweet princess, hath few minutes
    Remaining to run down; the sands are spent;   10
    For by an inward messenger I feel
    The summons of departure short and certain.

CALANTHA.
    You feed too much your melancholy.

4.1.] Calantha, Penthea *Q*.

---

9. *glass*] hourglass.
12. *short*] "early, near at hand" (*OED*).

PENTHEA.   Glories
    Of human greatness are but pleasing dreams
    And shadows soon decaying. On the stage   15
    Of my mortality, my youth hath acted
    Some scenes of vanity, drawn out at length
    By varied pleasures, sweeten'd in the mixture,
    But tragical in issue. Beauty, pomp,
    With every sensuality our giddiness   20
    Doth frame an idol, are unconstant friends
    When any troubled passion makes assault
    On the unguarded castle of the mind.
CALANTHA.
    Contemn not your condition for the proof
    Of bare opinion only. To what end   25
    Reach all these moral texts?
PENTHEA.   To place before 'ee
    A perfect mirror, wherein you may see
    How weary I am of a ling'ring life,
    Who count the best a misery.
CALANTHA.   Indeed
    You have no little cause, yet none so great   30
    As to distrust a remedy.
PENTHEA.   That remedy
    Must be a winding-sheet, a fold of lead,
    And some untrod-on corner in the earth.—
    Not to detain your expectation, princess,
    I have an humble suit.
CALANTHA.   Speak; I enjoy it.   35
PENTHEA.
    Vouchsafe then to be my executrix,
    And take that trouble on 'ee to dispose
    Such legacies as I bequeath impartially.
    I have not much to give, the pains are easy,
    Heaven will reward your piety and thank it   40
    When I am dead. For sure I must not live;
    I hope I cannot.

36. S.P. PENTHEA] *Weber; not in Q*.

24–25. *for . . . only*] i.e., on the basis of mere public opinion.

CALANTHA.   Now beshrew thy sadness;
  Thou turn'st me too much woman.
PENTHEA [*aside*].   Her fair eyes
  Melt into passion; then I have assurance
  Encouraging my boldness. —In this paper   45
  My will was character'd, which you, with pardon,
  Shall now know from mine own mouth.
CALANTHA.   Talk on, prithee;
  It is a pretty earnest.
PENTHEA.   I have left me
  But three poor jewels to bequeath. The first is
  My youth; for though I am much old in griefs,   50
  In years I am a child.
CALANTHA.   To whom that?
PENTHEA.
  To virgin wives, such as abuse not wedlock
  By freedom of desires, but covet chiefly
  The pledges of chaste beds for ties of love,
  Rather than ranging of their blood; and next   55
  To married maids, such as prefer the number
  Of honorable issue in their virtues
  Before the flattery of delights by marriage.
  May those be ever young.
CALANTHA.   A second jewel
  You mean to part with.
PENTHEA.   'Tis my fame, I trust   60
  By scandal yet untouch'd; this I bequeath
  To memory, and time's old daughter, truth.
  If ever my unhappy name find mention
  When I am fall'n to dust, may it deserve
  Beseeming charity without dishonor.   65
CALANTHA.
  How handsomely thou play'st with harmless sport
  Of mere imagination. Speak the last;
  I strangely like thy will.

---

43. *turn'st . . . woman*] make me weep.
46. *character'd*] written.
48. *earnest*] (1) pledge; (2) foretaste.
55. *ranging*] roving, straying.

PENTHEA.   This jewel, madam,
　　Is dearly precious to me; you must use
　　The best of your discretion to employ   70
　　This gift as I intend it.
CALANTHA.   Do not doubt me.
PENTHEA.
　　'Tis long agone since first I lost my heart.
　　Long I have liv'd without it, else for certain
　　I should have given that too. But instead
　　Of it, to great Calantha, Sparta's heir,   75
　　By service bound and by affection vow'd,
　　I do bequeath in holiest rites of love
　　Mine only brother, Ithocles.
CALANTHA.   What saidst thou?
PENTHEA.
　　Impute not, heaven-blest lady, to ambition
　　A faith as humbly perfect as the prayers   80
　　Of a devoted suppliant can endow it.
　　Look on him, princess, with an eye of pity;
　　How like the ghost of what he late appear'd
　　'A moves before you.
CALANTHA.   Shall I answer here,
　　Or lend my ear too grossly?
PENTHEA.   First, his heart   85
　　Shall fall in cinders, scorch'd by your disdain,
　　Ere he will dare, poor man, to ope an eye
　　On these divine looks, but with low-bent thoughts
　　Accusing such presumption. As for words,
　　'A dares not utter any but of service;   90
　　Yet this lost creature loves 'ee. Be a princess
　　In sweetness as in blood; give him his doom,
　　Or raise him up to comfort.
CALANTHA.   What new change
　　Appears in my behavior that thou dar'st
　　Tempt my displeasure?
PENTHEA.   I must leave the world   95
　　To revel in Elysium, and 'tis just
　　To wish my brother some advantage here.

96. in] *Weber; not in Q.*

Yet by my best hopes, Ithocles is ignorant
Of this pursuit. But if you please to kill him,
Lend him one angry look or one harsh word, 100
And you shall soon conclude how strong a power
Your absolute authority holds over
His life and end.

CALANTHA.   You have forgot, Penthea,
How still I have a father.

PENTHEA.   But remember
I am a sister, though to me this brother 105
Hath been, you know, unkind, O, most unkind!

CALANTHA.
Christalla, Philema, where are 'ee? —Lady,
Your check lies in my silence.

Enter Christalla *and* Philema.

BOTH.   Madam, here.

CALANTHA.
I think 'ee sleep, 'ee drones; wait on Penthea
Unto her lodging. —[*Aside.*]   Ithocles? Wrong'd lady! 110

PENTHEA.
My reckonings are made even. Death or fate
Can now nor strike too soon, nor force too late.   *Exeunt.*

[IV.i]   *Enter* Ithocles *and* Armostes.

ITHOCLES.
Forbear your inquisition. Curiosity
Is of too subtle and too searching nature,
In fears of love too quick, too slow of credit.
I am not what you doubt me.

ARMOSTES.   Nephew, be then
As I would wish. —[*Aside.*]   All is not right. —Good heaven 5
Confirm your resolutions for dependence
On worthy ends which may advance your quiet.

ITHOCLES.
I did the noble Orgilus much injury,

---

108. *check*] censure, reproof.
[IV.i]
   4. *doubt*] suspect.

But griev'd Penthea more. I now repent it;
Now, uncle, now. This "now" is now too late.   10
So provident is folly in sad issue
That after-wit, like bankrupts' debts, stand tallied
Without all possibilities of payment.
Sure he's an honest, very honest gentleman;
A man of single meaning.
ARMOSTES.   I believe it.   15
Yet nephew, 'tis the tongue informs our ears;
Our eyes can never pierce into the thoughts,
For they are lodg'd too inward. But I question
No truth in Orgilus. —The princess, sir.
ITHOCLES.
The princess? ha!
ARMOSTES.   With her the Prince of Argos.   20

Enter Nearchus, *leading* Calantha; Amelus, *Christalla, Philema.*

NEARCHUS.
Great fair one, grace my hopes with any instance
Of livery from the allowance of your favor;
This little spark—
CALANTHA.   A toy.
NEARCHUS.   Love feasts on toys,
For Cupid is a child. Vouchsafe this bounty;
It cannot be denied.
CALANTHA.   You shall not value,   25
Sweet cousin, at a price what I count cheap;
So cheap, that let him take it who dares stoop for't,
And give it at next meeting to a mistress.
She'll thank him for't, perhaps.   *Casts it to* Ithocles.
AMELUS.   The ring, sir, is
The princess's. I could have took it up.   30
ITHOCLES.
Learn manners, prithee. —To the blessed owner,
Upon my knees.
NEARCHUS.   Y'are saucy.

25. be denied] *Weber;* beny'd *Q.*

---

12. *after-wit*] wisdom that comes too late.
22. *livery*] personal article given to be worn as badge of service.

CALANTHA.   This is pretty.
　　I am, belike, a mistress! Wondrous pretty.
　　Let the man keep his fortune, since he found it;
　　He's worthy on't. —On, cousin.
ITHOCLES.   Follow, spaniel;   35
　　I'll force 'ee to a fawning else.
AMELUS.   You dare not.
　　　　　　　　　　　Exeunt. Manent Ithocles *and* Armostes.
ARMOSTES.
　　My lord, you were too forward.
ITHOCLES.   Look 'ee, uncle,
　　Some such there are whose liberal contents
　　Swarm without care in every sort of plenty;
　　Who, after full repasts, can lay them down   40
　　To sleep. And they sleep, uncle; in which silence
　　Their very dreams present 'em choice of pleasures,
　　Pleasures (observe me, uncle) of rare object:
　　Here heaps of gold, there increments of honors,
　　Now change of garments, then the votes of people,   45
　　Anon varieties of beauties, courting
　　In flatteries of the night, exchange of dalliance.
　　Yet these are still but dreams. Give me felicity
　　Of which my senses waking are partakers,
　　A real, visible, material happiness;   50
　　And then too, when I stagger in expectance
　　Of the least comfort that can cherish life.
　　I saw it, sir, I saw it; for it came
　　From her own hand.
ARMOSTES.   The princess threw it t'ee.
ITHOCLES.
　　True, and she said—well I remember what.   55
　　Her cousin prince would beg it.
ARMOSTES.   Yes, and parted
　　In anger at your taking on't.
ITHOCLES.   Penthea!
　　O, thou hast pleaded with a powerful language.
　　I want a fee to gratify thy merit.

59. merit] *Weber;* myrit *Q.*

---

32. *pretty*] ingenious, clever.

But I will do—

ARMOSTES.   What is't you say?

ITHOCLES.   In anger,   60
In anger let him part; for could his breath,
Like whirlwinds, toss such servile slaves as lick
The dust his footsteps print, into a vapor,
It durst not stir a hair of mine. It should not,
I'd rend it up by th' roots first. To be anything   65
Calantha smiles on is to be a blessing
More sacred than a petty prince of Argos
Can wish to equal, or in worth or title.

ARMOSTES.
Contain yourself, my lord. Ixion, aiming
To embrace Juno, bosom'd but a cloud   70
And begat centaurs. 'Tis an useful moral:
Ambition, hatch'd in clouds of mere opinion,
Proves but in birth a prodigy.

ITHOCLES.   I thank 'ee;
Yet, with your license, I should seem uncharitable
To gentler fate, if relishing the dainties   75
Of a soul's settled peace, I were so feeble
Not to digest it.

ARMOSTES.   He deserves small trust
Who is not privy counsellor to himself.

Enter Nearchus, Orgilus, *and* Amelus.

NEARCHUS.
Brave me?

ORGILUS.   Your excellence mistakes his temper,
For Ithocles in fashion of his mind   80
Is beautiful, soft, gentle, the clear mirror
Of absolute perfection.

AMELUS.   Was't your modesty
Term'd any of the prince his servants "spaniel"?
Your nurse sure taught you other language.

ITHOCLES.   Language!

NEARCHUS.
A gallant man at arms is here, a doctor   85

70. *bosom'd*] embraced.
73. *prodigy*] monster.

In feats of chivalry, blunt and rough-spoken,
Vouchsafing not the fustian of civility,
Which less rash spirits style good manners.

ITHOCLES.   Manners!

ORGILUS.

No more, illustrious sir; 'tis matchless Ithocles.

NEARCHUS.

You might have understood who I am.

ITHOCLES.   Yes,   90
I did; else—but the presence calm'd th'affront—
Y'are cousin to the princess.

NEARCHUS.   To the king too,
A certain instrument that lent supportance
To your colossic greatness; to that king too,
You might have added.

ITHOCLES.   There is more divinity   95
In beauty than in majesty.

ARMOSTES.   O fie, fie!

NEARCHUS.

This odd youth's pride turns heretic in loyalty.—
Sirrah, low mushrooms never rival cedars.

                                Exeunt Nearchus *and* Amelus.

ITHOCLES.

Come back! What pitiful dull thing am I
So to be tamely scolded at. Come back!   100
Let him come back and echo once again
That scornful sound of "mushroom"; painted colts,
Like heralds' coats gilt o'er with crowns and scepters,
May bait a muzzled lion.

---

88. less] *Gifford; not in Q.*   104. muzzled] *Weber;* musled *Q.*

---

87. *fustian*] inflated, pompous language; bombast.
91. *presence*] i.e., of royalty.
98. *mushrooms*] here probably signifying "upstart," a connotation derived from the rapid growth of the plant.
98. *cedars*] The cedar, praised in the Old Testament for its majestic loftiness, often symbolizes in Renaissance literature royal or eminent persons; cf. Tilley, C 206 and C 207.
102–104. *painted . . . lion*] "It was a popular belief that lions were afraid of virgins, cocks, and the royal blood; a herald's coat adorned with the king's insignia might be presumed to have the same awe-inspiring power" (Sherman). For *muzzled lion*, Ford's use of heraldry may be even more direct; a muzzled bear, at least, appears on some coats of arms.

ARMOSTES.   Cousin, cousin,
    Thy tongue is not thy friend.
ORGILUS.   In point of honor   105
    Discretion knows no bounds. Amelus told me
    'Twas all about a little ring.
ITHOCLES.   A ring
    The princess threw away, and I took up.
    Admit she threw't to me, what arm of brass
    Can snatch it hence? No, could 'a grind the hoop   110
    To powder, 'a might sooner reach my heart
    Than steal and wear one dust on't. Orgilus,
    I am extremely wrong'd.
ORGILUS.   A lady's favor
    Is not to be so slighted.
ITHOCLES.   Slighted!
ARMOSTES.   Quiet
    These vain unruly passions, which will render ye   115
    Into a madness.
ORGILUS.   Griefs will have their vent.

Enter Tecnicus.

ARMOSTES.
    Welcome; thou com'st in season, reverend man,
    To pour the balsam of a suppling patience
    Into the festering wound of ill-spent fury.
ORGILUS [*aside*].
    What makes he here?
TECNICUS.   The hurts are yet but mortal   120
    Which shortly will prove deadly. To the king,
    Armostes, see in safety thou deliver
    This seal'd up counsel; bid him with a constancy
    Peruse the secrets of the gods. —O Sparta,
    O Lacedemon! double-nam'd, but one   125
    In fate. When kingdoms reel (mark well my saw)

104. Cousin, cousin] *Weber;* Cozen,   118. suppling] *Dyce;* supplying *Q.*
Coxen *Q.*

---

   118. *balsam*] "an aromatic oily resinous preparation, usually for external
application, for healing wounds or soothing pain" (*OED*).
   118. *suppling*] healing.
   120. *mortal*] "doomed to immediate death" (*OED*).

Their heads must needs be giddy. —Tell the king
That henceforth he no more must inquire after
My aged head; Apollo wills it so.
I am for Delphos.

ARMOSTES.   Not without some conference   130
With our great master?

TECNICUS.   Never more to see him;
A greater prince commands me. —Ithocles,
When youth is ripe and age from time doth part,
The lifeless trunk shall wed the broken heart.

ITHOCLES.
What's this, if understood?

TECNICUS.   List, Orgilus;   135
Remember what I told thee long before,
These tears shall be my witness.

ARMOSTES.   'Las, good man.

TECNICUS.
Let craft with courtesy a while confer,
Revenge proves its own executioner.

ORGILUS.
Dark sentences are for Apollo's priests.   140
I am not Oedipus.

TECNICUS.   My hour is come;
Cheer up the king. Farewell to all. —O Sparta,
O Lacedemon!   *Exit* Tecn[icus].

ARMOSTES.   If prophetic fire
Have warm'd this old man's bosom, we might construe
His words to fatal sense.

ITHOCLES.   Leave to the powers   145
Above us the effects of their decrees;
My burden lies within me. Servile fears
Prevent no great effects. —Divine Calantha!

ARMOSTES.
The gods be still propitious.   *Exeunt; manet* Orgilus.

ORGILUS.   Something oddly
The book-man prated, yet 'a talk'd it weeping: 150
Let craft with courtesy a while confer,

---

141. *Oedipus*] He solved the riddle of the Sphinx and thereby saved
Thebes from distress.

Revenge proves its own executioner.
Con it again; for what? It shall not puzzle me;
'Tis dotage of a withered brain. —Penthea
Forbade me not her presence; I may see her   155
And gaze my fill. Why see her then I may;
When if I faint to speak, I must be silent.   *Exit* Orgilus.

[IV.ii]   *Enter* Bassanes, Grausis, *and* Phulas.

BASSANES.

Pray use your recreations; all the service
I will expect is quietness amongst 'ee.
Take liberty at home, abroad, at all times,
And in your charities appease the gods,
Whom I with my distractions have offended.   5

'GRAUSIS.

Fair blessings on thy heart.

PHULAS [*aside*].   Here's a rare change.
My lord, to cure the itch, is surely gelded;
The cuckold in conceit hath cast his horns.

BASSANES.

Betake 'ee to your several occasions,
And wherein I have heretofore been faulty   10
Let your constructions mildly pass it over.
Henceforth I'll study reformation. More
I have not for employment.

GRAUSIS.   O sweet man,
Thou art the very honeycomb of honesty!

PHULAS.

The garland of good will. —Old lady, hold up   15
Thy reverend snout and trot behind me softly,

---

8. *conceit*] imagination.

9. *several occasions*] various activities.

11. *constructions*] interpretations.

14–15. *honeycomb .... good will*] *A Garland of Goodwill* (1576) was a
popular collection of ballads, many of them about the amours of English
kings; another edition appeared in 1629. The term *honeycomb* was used to
signify a collection of religious or philosophical sayings, as *The honey-combe
of free justification by Christ alone Collected out of the meere authorities of Scripture*
(1642), by Joah Eaton (fl. 1619).

16–17. *trot ... ancient*] *Old trot* was "a name of ridicule and contempt for
a decrepit old woman" (Nares).

As it becomes a moil of ancient carriage.

Exeunt; manet Bassanes.

BASSANES.

Beasts, only capable of sense, enjoy
The benefit of food and ease with thankfulness;
Such silly creatures with a grudging kick not   20
Against the portion nature hath bestow'd.
But men, endow'd with reason, and the use
Of reason, to distinguish from the chaff
Of abject scarcity the quintessence,
Soul, and elixir of the earth's abundance,   25
The treasures of the sea, the air, nay, heaven,
Repining at these glories of creation,
Are verier beasts than beasts. And of those beasts
The worst am I: I, who was made a monarch
Of what a heart could wish for, a chaste wife,   30
Endeavor'd what in me lay to pull down
That temple built for adoration only,
And level't in the dust of causeless scandal.
But, to redeem a sacrilege so impious,
Humility shall pour, before the deities   35
I have incens'd, a largess of more patience
Than their displeased altars can require.
No tempests of commotion shall disquiet
The calms of my composure.

Enter Orgilus.

ORGILUS.   I have found thee,
Thou patron of more horrors than the bulk   40
Of manhood, hoop'd about with ribs of iron,
Can cram within thy breast. Penthea, Bassanes,
Curs'd by thy jealousies—more, by thy dotage—
Is left a prey to words.

36. largess] *Weber;* largenesse *Q.*

17. *moil*] mule.
24. *quintessence*] "a term much used by alchemists. The fifth essence, which the Greeks who were followers of Pythagoras added to the four recognized elements, fire, air, water, and earth" (Scollard).
40. *bulk*] (1) body, trunk; (2) hull of a ship (*OED*).
44. *words*] scandal.

BASSANES.   Exercise

   Your trials for addition to my penance;   45

   I am resolv'd.

ORGILUS.   Play not with misery

   Past cure. Some angry minister of fate hath

   Depos'd the empress of her soul, her reason,

   From its most proper throne; but what's the miracle

   More new, I, I have seen it, and yet live.   50

BASSANES.

   You may delude my senses, not my judgment.

   'Tis anchor'd into a firm resolution;

   Dalliance of mirth or wit can ne'er unfix it.

   Practice yet further.

ORGILUS.   May thy death of love to her

   Damn all thy comforts to a lasting fast   55

   From every joy of life. Thou barren rock,

   By thee we have been split in ken of harbor.

Enter Ithocles; Penthea, *her hair about her ears;* Philema; Christalla.

ITHOCLES.

   Sister, look up; your Ithocles, your brother

   Speaks t'ee. Why do you weep? Dear, turn not from me.—

   Here is a killing sight: lo, Bassanes,   60

   A lamentable object.

ORGILUS.   Man, dost see't?

   Sports are more gamesome; am I yet in merriment?

   Why dost not laugh?

BASSANES.   Divine and best of ladies,

   Please to forget my outrage. Mercy ever

   Cannot but lodge under a roof so excellent.   65

   I have cast off that cruelty of frenzy

   Which once appear'd impostors and then juggled

   To cheat my sleeps of rest.

ORGILUS.   Was I in earnest?

PENTHEA.

   Sure if we were all sirens we should sing pitifully,

57. been] *Weber;* bee *Q*.   65. roof] *Weber;* root *Q*.

---

   54. *Practice yet further*] "i.e., try all your vexations upon me" (Gifford).

   57. *ken*] sight.

   69. *sirens*] "Fabulous monsters, part woman, part bird, who were supposed to lure sailors to destruction by their enchanting song" (*OED*).

And 'twere a comely music when in parts   70
One sung another's knell. The turtle sighs
When he hath lost his mate, and yet some say
'A must be dead first. 'Tis a fine deceit
To pass away in a dream. Indeed I've slept
With mine eyes open a great while. No falsehood   75
Equals a broken faith. There's not a hair
Sticks on my head but like a leaden plummet
It sinks me to the grave. I must creep thither;
The journey is not long.

ITHOCLES.   But thou, Penthea,
Hast many years, I hope, to number yet   80
Ere thou canst travel that way.

BASSANES.   Let the sun first
Be wrapp'd up in an everlasting darkness,
Before the light of nature, chiefly form'd
For the whole world's delight, feel an eclipse
So universal.

ORGILUS.   Wisdom, look 'ee,   85
Begins to rave. —Art thou mad too, antiquity?

PENTHEA.

Since I was first a wife, I might have been
Mother to many pretty prattling babes.
They would have smil'd when I smil'd; and, for certain,
I should have cried when they cried; truly, brother,   90
My father would have pick'd me out a husband,
And then my little ones had been no bastards.
But 'tis too late for me to marry now,

81. sun] *Weber;* Swan *Q.*

71–72. *turtle . . . mate*] proverbial; cf. Tilley, T 624. In *The Winter's Tale* (V.iii.132–135), Paulina says: "I, an old turtle,/ Will wing me to some wither'd bough, and there/ My mate, that's never to be found again,/ Lament till I am lost."

74–75. *I've . . . while*] in Ford's *The Lover's Melancholy*, Trollio says of Meleander, "he sleeps like a hare, with his eyes open, and that's no good sign" (II.ii). Penthea has not slept for ten days (IV.ii.135); Burton, in *The Anatomy of Melancholy* (Part. 1, Sect. 3, Memb. 1, Subs. 1), cites sleeplessness as a symptom of melancholy: "they cannot sleep, they have mighty and often watchings, sometimes working for a month, a year, together . . . . Trincavellius speaks of one that waked 50 days, and Sckenkius hath examples of two years."

I am past child-bearing; 'tis not my fault.

BASSANES.

    Fall on me, if there be a burning Aetna,   95
    And bury me in flames! Sweats hot as sulphur
    Boil through my pores! Affliction hath in store
    No torture like to this.

ORGILUS.   Behold a patience!—
    Lay by thy whining gray dissimulation,
    Do something worth a chronicle. Show justice   100
    Upon the author of this mischief; dig out
    The jealousies that hatch'd this thralldom first
    With thine own poniard. Every antic rapture
    Can roar as thine does.

ITHOCLES.   Orgilus, forbear.

BASSANES.

    Disturb him not, it is a talking motion   105
    Provided for my torment. What a fool am I
    To bandy passion. Ere I'll speak a word,
    I will look on and burst.

PENTHEA.   I lov'd you once.

ORGILUS.

    Thou didst, wrong'd creature; in despite of malice,
    For it I love thee ever.

PENTHEA.   Spare your hand;   110
    Believe me, I'll not hurt it.

ORGILUS.   Pain my heart too.

PENTHEA.

    Complain not though I wring it hard. I'll kiss it;
    O, 'tis a fine soft palm. Hark, in thine ear,
    Like whom do I look, prithee? Nay, no whispering.
    Goodness! we had been happy; too much happiness   115
    Will make folk proud, they say—but that is he;

                          Points at Ithocles.

    And yet he paid for't home. Alas, his heart

---

107. bandy] *Dyce;* bawdy *Q.*   112. S.P. PENTHEA] *Weber; not in Q.*
111. too] *Weber;* to *Q.*

  95. *Aetna*] volcano in northeast Sicily.
  103. *antic*] uncouthly ludicrous.   105. *talking motion*] puppet.

Is crept into the cabinet of the princess;
We shall have points and bride-laces. Remember
When we last gather'd roses in the garden;   120
I found my wits, but truly you lost yours.
That's he, and still 'tis he.

ITHOCLES.   Poor soul, how idly
Her fancies guide her tongue.

BASSANES.   Keep in vexation,
And break not into clamor.

ORGILUS.   She has tutor'd me;
Some powerful inspiration checks my laziness.—   125
Now let me kiss your hand, griev'd beauty.

PENTHEA.   Kiss it.—
Alack, alack, his lips be wondrous cold;
Dear soul, h'as lost his color. Have 'ee seen
A straying heart? All crannies! every drop
Of blood is turn'd to an amethyst,   130
Which married bachelors hang in their ears.

ORGILUS.
Peace usher her into Elysium.
If this be madness, madness is an oracle.   *Exit* Orgilus.

ITHOCLES.
Christalla, Philema, when slept my sister,
Her ravings are so wild?

CHRISTALLA.   Sir, not these ten days.   135

PHILEMA.
We watch by her continually; besides,
We cannot any way pray her to eat.

BASSANES.
O misery of miseries!

PENTHEA.   Take comfort,
You may live well and die a good old man.
By yea and nay, an oath not to be broken,   140
If you had join'd our hands once in the temple—

---

119. *points*] "tagged laces, used in dress" (Dyce).
119. *bride-laces*] "pieces of silk or lace used to tie the sprigs of rosemary in use at weddings" (Spencer).
122. *idly*] incoherently.

−79−

'Twas since my father died, for had he liv'd
He would have done't—I must have call'd you father.
O, my wrack'd honor, ruin'd by those tyrants,
A cruel brother and a desperate dotage!   145
There is no peace left for a ravish'd wife
Widow'd by lawless marriage; to all memory
Penthea's, poor Penthea's name is strumpeted.
But since her blood was season'd by the forfeit
Of noble shame with mixtures of pollution,   150
Her blood ('tis just) be henceforth never heighten'd
With taste of sustenance. Starve; let that fullness
Whose pleurisy hath fever'd faith and modesty—
Forgive me. O, I faint!

ARMOSTES.   Be not so willful,
Sweet niece, to work thine own destruction.

ITHOCLES.   Nature   155
Will call her daughter monster. —What! not eat?
Refuse the only ordinary means
Which are ordain'd for life? Be not, my sister,
A murd'ress to thyself. —Hear'st thou this, Bassanes?

BASSANES.
Foh! I am busy; for I have not thoughts   160
Enow to think. All shall be well anon;
'Tis tumbling in my head: there is a mastery
In art to fatten and keep smooth the outside,
Yes, and to comfort up the vital spirits
Without the help of food; fumes or perfumes,   165
Perfumes or fumes. Let her alone; I'll search out
The trick on't.

PENTHEA.   Lead me gently; heavens reward ye.
Griefs are sure friends; they leave without control
Nor cure nor comforts for a leprous soul.

                    Exeunt the maids supporting Penthea.

---

153. *pleurisy*] excess.

162–167. *there . . . . on't*] "There is a contemporary ballad in the Shirburn
collection 'Of a maide now dwelling at the towne of *meurs* in *dutchland*,
that hath not taken any foode this 16 yeares, and is not yet neither hungry
nor thirsty; the which maide hath lately beene presented to the lady
elizabeth, the king's daughter of england.' This 'maide' subsisted in the
manner proposed by Bassanes—on perfumes" (Sherman).

BASSANES.

 I grant t'ee, and will put in practice instantly   170
 What you shall still admire. 'Tis wonderful,
 'Tis super-singular, not to be match'd.
 Yet when I've done't, I've done't; ye shall all thank me.

              Exit Bassanes.

ARMOSTES.

 The sight is full of terror.

ITHOCLES.   On my soul

 Lies such an infinite clog of massy dullness   175
 As that I have not sense enough to feel it.
 See, uncle, th'augury thing returns again;
 Shall's welcome him with thunder? We are haunted,
 And must use exorcism to conjure down
 This spirit of malevolence.

ARMOSTES.   Mildly, nephew.   180

      Enter Nearchus *and* Amelus.

NEARCHUS.

 I come not, sir, to chide your late disorder,
 Admitting that th'inurement to a roughness
 In soldiers of your years and fortunes, chiefly
 So lately prosperous, hath not yet shook off
 The custom of the war in hours of leisure.   185
 Nor shall you need excuse, since y'are to render
 Account to that fair excellence the princess,
 Who in her private gallery expects it
 From your own mouth alone. I am a messenger
 But to her pleasure.

ITHOCLES.   Excellent Nearchus,   190

 Be prince still of my services, and conquer
 Without the combat of dispute; I honor 'ee.

NEARCHUS.

 The king is on a sudden indispos'd,
 Physicians are call'd for; 'twere fit, Armostes,

---

 171. *admire*] wonder at.

 175. *clog*] encumbrance, hindrance. A clog, literally, was "a heavy piece of wood attached to leg or neck of man or beast, to impede motion or prevent escape" (*OED*).

 181. *disorder*] disorderly conduct.

You should be near him.

ARMOSTES.   Sir, I kiss your hands.   195

Exeunt. Manent Nearchus *and* Amelus.

NEARCHUS.

Amelus, I perceive Calantha's bosom
Is warm'd with other fires than such as can
Take strength from any fuel of the love
I might address to her. Young Ithocles,
Or ever I mistake, is lord ascendant   200
Of her devotions; one, to speak him truly,
In every disposition nobly fashioned.

AMELUS.

But can your highness brook to be so rival'd,
Considering th'inequality of the persons?

NEARCHUS.

I can, Amelus; for affections injur'd   205
By tyranny or rigor of compulsion,
Like tempest-threaten'd trees unfirmly rooted,
Ne'er spring to timely growth. Observe, for instance,
Life-spent Penthea and unhappy Orgilus.

AMELUS.

How does your grace determine?

NEARCHUS.   To be jealous   210
In public of what privately I'll further;
And though they shall not know, yet they shall find it.

Exeunt omnes.

[IV.iii]

Enter Hemophil *and* Groneas, *leading* Amyclas *and placing him in a
chair, followed by* Armostes, Crotolon, *and* Prophilus.

AMYCLAS.

Our daughter is not near?

---

200. *lord ascendant*] an astrological term, here signifying figuratively that
Calantha loves Ithocles. The *ascendant* is "the point of the ecliptic, or degree
of the zodiac, which at any moment (esp. *e.g.* at the birth of a child) is just
rising above the eastern horizon; the horoscope. *The house of the ascendant*
includes 5 degrees of the zodiac above this point and 25 below it. *The
lord of the ascendant*: any planet within the house of the ascendant. (The
ascendant and its lord were supposed to exercise a special influence upon the
life of a child then born)" (*OED*).

ARMOSTES.   She is retired, sir,
    Into her gallery.
AMYCLAS.   Where's the prince our cousin?
PROPHILUS.
    New walk'd into the grove, my lord.
AMYCLAS.   All leave us
    Except Armostes and you, Crotolon;
    We would be private.
PROPHILUS.   Health unto your majesty.   5
                    Exeunt Prophilus, Hemophil, *and* Groneas.
AMYCLAS.
    What, Tecnicus is gone?
ARMOSTES.   He is to Delphos,
    And to your royal hands presents this box.
AMYCLAS.
    Unseal it, good Armostes; therein lies
    The secrets of the oracle. Out with it.
    Apollo live our patron! Read, Armostes.   10
ARMOSTES.
    The plot in which the vine takes root
    Begins to dry from head to foot;
    The stock soon withering, want of sap
    Doth cause to quail the budding grape.
    But from the neighboring elm a dew   15
    Shall drop and feed the plot anew.
AMYCLAS.
    That is the oracle; what exposition
    Makes the philosopher?
ARMOSTES.   This brief one only:
    The plot is Sparta, the dried vine the king,
    The quailing grape his daughter; but the thing   20
    Of most importance, not to be reveal'd,
    Is a near prince, the elm; the rest conceal'd.
                                    Tecnicus.
AMYCLAS.
    Enough; although the opening of this riddle
    Be but itself a riddle, yet we construe

---

14. *quail*] wither.
23. *opening*] expounding, interpretation.

How near our lab'ring age draws to a rest.   25
But must Calantha quail too, that young grape
Untimely budded? I could mourn for her;
Her tenderness hath yet deserv'd no rigor
So to be cross'd by fate.

ARMOSTES.   You misapply, sir—
With favor let me speak it—what Apollo   30
Hath clouded in hid sense: I here conjecture
Her marriage with some neighb'ring prince, the dew
Of which befriending elm shall ever strengthen
Your subjects with a sovereignty of power.

CROTOLON.

Besides, most gracious lord, the pith of oracles   35
Is to be then digested when th'events
Expound their truth, not brought as soon to light
As utter'd; truth is child of time, and herein
I find no scruple, rather cause of comfort
With unity of kingdoms.

AMYCLAS.   May it prove so,   40
For weal of this dear nation. —Where is Ithocles?—
Armostes, Crotolon, when this wither'd vine
Of my frail carcass on the funeral pile
Is fir'd into its ashes, let that young man
Be hedg'd about still with your cares and loves;   45
Much owe I to his worth, much to his service.—
Let such as wait come in now.

ARMOSTES.   All attend here.

Enter Ithocles, Calantha, Prophilus, Orgilus, Euphranea, Hemophil, *and* Groneas.

CALANTHA.

Dear sir, king, father!

ITHOCLES.   O my royal master!

AMYCLAS.

Cleave not my heart, sweet twins of my life's solace,
With your forejudging fears. There is no physic   50
So cunningly restorative to cherish

26. too] *Gifford;* to *Q.*

---

51. *cherish*] (1) treat with fostering care; (2) cheer, encourage (*OED*).

The fall of age, or call back youth and vigor,
As your consents in duty. I will shake off
This languishing disease of time, to quicken
Fresh pleasures in these drooping hours of sadness.   55
Is fair Euphranea married yet to Prophilus?

CROTOLON.

This morning, gracious lord.

ORGILUS.   This very morning;
Which, with your highness' leave, you may observe too.
Our sister looks, methinks, mirthful and sprightly,
As if her chaster fancy could already   60
Expound the riddle of her gain in losing
A trifle; maids know only that they know not.
Pish! prithee blush not; 'tis but honest change
Of fashion in the garment, loose for strait,
And so the modest maid is made a wife.   65
Shrewd business, is't not, sister?

EUPHRANEA.   You are pleasant.

AMYCLAS.

We thank thee, Orgilus; this mirth becomes thee.
But wherefore sits the court in such a silence?
A wedding without revels is not seemly.

CALANTHA.

Your late indisposition, sir, forbade it.   70

AMYCLAS.

Be it thy charge, Calantha, to set forward
The bridal sports, to which I will be present;
If not, at least consenting. —Mine own Ithocles,
I have done little for thee yet.

ITHOCLES.   Y'have built me
To the full height I stand in.

CALANTHA [aside].   Now or never!—   75
May I propose a suit?

AMYCLAS.   Demand and have it.

CALANTHA.

Pray sir, give me this young man, and no further
Account him yours than he deserves in all things
To be thought worthy mine; I will esteem him
According to his merit.

AMYCLAS.   Still th'art my daughter,   80

Still grow'st upon my heart.—[*To* Ithocles.] Give me thine hand;
Calantha, take thine own. In noble actions
Thou'lt find him firm and absolute. —I would not
Have parted with thee, Ithocles, to any
But to a mistress who is all what I am.   85

ITHOCLES.

A change, great king, most wish'd for 'cause the same.

CALANTHA.

Th'art mine. —[*Aside to* Ithocles.]   Have I now kept my
                                                        word?

ITHOCLES [*aside to* Calantha].   Divinely.

ORGILUS.

Rich fortunes, guard to favor of a princess,
Rock thee, brave man, in ever-crowned plenty;
Y'are minion of the time, be thankful for it.—   90
[*Aside.*]   Ho, here's a swinge in destiny! apparent,
The youth is up on tiptoe, yet may stumble.

AMYCLAS.

On to your recreations. —Now convey me
Unto my bedchamber. —None on his forehead
Wear a distempered look.

OMNES.   The gods preserve 'ee.   95

CALANTHA [*aside to* Ithocles].

Sweet, be not from my sight.

ITHOCLES [*aside to* Calantha].   My whole felicity!
              Exeunt, carrying out of the king; Orgilus stays Ithocles.

ORGILUS.

Shall I be bold, my lord?

ITHOCLES.   Thou canst not, Orgilus.
Call me thine own, for Prophilus must henceforth
Be all thy sister's; friendship, though it cease not
In marriage, yet is oft at less command   100
Than when a single freedom can dispose it.

ORGILUS.

Most right, my most good lord, my most great lord,

---

95. Wear] *Weber;* Were *Q*.

---

90. *minion*] favorite.
91. *swinge*] "sway, power, rule, authority, influence" (*OED*).

My gracious princely lord, I might add, royal.
ITHOCLES.
    Royal? A subject royal?
ORGILUS.   Why not, pray sir?
    The sovereignty of kingdoms in their nonage   105
    Stoop'd to desert, not birth; there's as much merit
    In clearness of affection as in puddle
    Of generation. You have conquer'd love
    Even in the loveliest; if I greatly err not,
    The son of Venus hath bequeath'd his quiver   110
    To Ithocles his manage, by whose arrows
    Calantha's breast is open'd.
ITHOCLES.   Can 't be possible?
ORGILUS.
    I was myself a piece of suitor once,
    And forward in preferment too; so forward
    That, speaking truth, I may without offence, sir,   115
    Presume to whisper that my hopes and, hark 'ee,
    My certainty of marriage stood assured
    With as firm footing, by your leave, as any's
    Now at this very instant—but—
ITHOCLES.   'Tis granted.
    And for a league of privacy between us,   120
    Read o'er my bosom and partake a secret:
    The princess is contracted mine.
ORGILUS.   Still, why not?
    I now applaud her wisdom; when your kingdom
    Stands seated in your will secure and settled,
    I dare pronounce you will be a just monarch.   125
    Greece must admire and tremble.
ITHOCLES.   Then the sweetness
    Of so imparadis'd a comfort, Orgilus!
    It is to banquet with the gods.
ORGILUS.   The glory
    Of numerous children, potency of nobles,
    Bent knees, hearts pav'd to tread on.

---

    107. *clearness . . . affection*] purity of disposition.
    107–108. *puddle . . . generation*] the confusion or muddle resulting from descent.

ITHOCLES.   With a friendship   130
    So dear, so fast as thine.
ORGILUS.   I am unfitting
    For office, but for service.
ITHOCLES.   We'll distinguish
    Our fortunes merely in the title, partners
    In all respects else but the bed.
ORGILUS.   The bed?
    Forfend it, Jove's own jealousy!—till lastly   135
    We slip down in the common earth together;
    And there our beds are equal, save some monument
    To show this was the king, and this the subject.—

                                            Soft sad music.
    List, what sad sounds are these? Extremely sad ones.
ITHOCLES.
    Sure from Penthea's lodgings.
ORGILUS.   Hark, a voice too.   140

                        A song [within].
            O no more, no more; too late
            Sighs are spent. The burning tapers
            Of a life as chaste as fate,
            Pure as are unwritten papers,
                Are burnt out. No heat, no light   145
                Now remains; 'tis ever night.
            Love is dead; let lovers' eyes,
                Lock'd in endless dreams,
                Th'extremes of all extremes,
            Ope no more, for now love dies,   150
                Now love dies, implying
            Love's martyrs must be ever, ever dying.

ITHOCLES.
    O my misgiving heart!
ORGILUS.   A horrid stillness
    Succeeds this deathful air; let's know the reason.
    Tread softly; there is mystery in mourning.   *Exeunt.* 155

138.1.] *Q prints on l. 140.1.*

[IV.iv]

Enter Christalla *and* Philema, *bringing in* Penthea *in a chair, veil'd; two other* Servants *placing two chairs, one on the one side, and the other with an engine on the other. The* Maids *sit down at her feet, mourning. The* Servants *go out; meet them* Ithocles *and* Orgilus.

SERVANT [*aside to* Orgilus].
 'Tis done, that on her right hand.
ORGILUS.   Good, begone.
ITHOCLES.
 Soft peace enrich this room.
ORGILUS.   How fares the lady?
PHILEMA.
 Dead.
CHRISTALLA. Dead.
PHILEMA.   Starv'd.
CHRISTALLA.   Starv'd.
ITHOCLES.   Me miserable!
ORGILUS.   Tell us,
 How parted she from life?
PHILEMA.   She call'd for music,
 And begg'd some gentle voice to tune a farewell   5
 To life and griefs. Christalla touch'd the lute,

0.3. *engine*] For this device Ford probably is indebted to *The Devil's Charter* (1606) by Barnabe Barnes, for whose *Foure Bookes of Offices* (1606) Ford wrote commendatory verses. Gifford comments: "This *engine* . . . was merely a couple of movable arms added to the common chair. The contrivance is of early date . . . . Vulcan, he [Pausanias] tells us, in order to be revenged of Juno for turning him out of heaven, insidiously presented her with a golden throne with hidden springs, which prevented her, after being seated upon it, from rising up again . . . . Ford, however, brought no golden chair from Olympus: he found his simple contrivance not only on the stage, but in Bandello (Nov. 27, part iv), where . . . Deodati is entrapped by il Turchi, precisely as Ithocles is here by Orgilus, and then stabbed with a dagger. . . . [Barnes appears] to have been aware of the passage in Pausanias:—but he evidently was a scholar; 'Enter Lucretia with a *chair* in her hand, which she sets on the stage' . . . . And accordingly Gismond sits down, is 'grasped,' like Ithocles, and stabbed without resistance by his wife; who retires, as she entered, 'with the *chair* in her hand.'" Pepys, in his *Diary* (entry for Nov. 1, 1660), describes Sir William Batten's "King Harry's Chair, where he that sits down is catched with two irons, that come round about him."

I wept the funeral song.

CHRISTALLA.   Which scarce was ended
But her last breath seal'd up these hollow sounds,
"O cruel Ithocles and injur'd Orgilus!"
So down she drew her veil, so died.

ITHOCLES.   So died!   10

ORGILUS.

Up; you are messengers of death, go from us;
Here's woe enough to court without a prompter.
Away; and hark ye, till you see us next,
No syllable that she is dead. Away,
Keep a smooth brow.   *Exeunt* Philema *and* Christalla.
               —My lord—

ITHOCLES.   Mine only sister,   15
Another is not left me.

ORGILUS.   Take that chair,
I'll seat me here in this; between us sits
The object of our sorrows. Some few tears
We'll part among us; I perhaps can mix
One lamentable story to prepare 'em.   20
There, there, sit there, my lord.

ITHOCLES.   Yes, as you please.

          Ithocles *sits down, and is catch'd in the engine.*

What means this treachery?

ORGILUS.   Caught! You are caught,
Young master; 'tis thy throne of coronation,
Thou fool of greatness. See, I take this veil off;
Survey a beauty wither'd by the flames   25
Of an insulting Phaeton, her brother.

ITHOCLES.

Thou mean'st to kill me basely.

ORGILUS.   I foreknew
The last act of her life, and train'd thee hither
To sacrifice a tyrant to a turtle.
You dreamt of kingdoms, did 'ee? How to bosom   30
The delicacies of a youngling princess,

15. S.D.] Q *prints on l. 14.*

---

28. *train'd*] lured.

How with this nod to grace that subtle courtier,
How with that frown to make this noble tremble,
And so forth; whiles Penthea's groans and tortures,
Her agonies, her miseries, afflictions   35
Ne'er touch'd upon your thought. As for my injuries,
Alas they were beneath your royal pity,
But yet they liv'd, thou proud man, to confound thee.
Behold thy fate, this steel.   [*Draws a dagger.*]
ITHOCLES.   Strike home; a courage
As keen as thy revenge shall give it welcome.   40
But prithee faint not; if the wound close up,
Tent it with double force and search it deeply.
Thou look'st that I should whine and beg compassion,
As loath to leave the vainness of my glories;
A statelier resolution arms my confidence,   45
To cozen thee of honor. Neither could I,
With equal trial of unequal fortune,
By hazard of a duel; 'twere a bravery
Too mighty for a slave intending murder.
On to the execution, and inherit   50
A conflict with thy horrors.
ORGILUS.   By Apollo,
Thou talk'st a goodly language. For requital,
I will report thee to thy mistress richly.
And take this peace along: some few short minutes
Determin'd, my resolves shall quickly follow   55
Thy wrathful ghost; then if we tug for mastery,
Penthea's sacred eyes shall lend new courage.
Give me thy hand, be healthful in thy parting
From lost mortality. Thus, thus, I free it.   *Kills him.*
ITHOCLES.
Yet, yet, I scorn to shrink.
ORGILUS.   Keep up thy spirit.   60
I will be gentle even in blood; to linger

---

42. *Tent*] probe; from the noun *tent*, "a roll of lint employed in examining
or purifying a deep wound" (Nares).
48. *bravery*] (1) bravado; (2) act of courage.
55. *Determin'd*] terminated.
61. *linger*] prolong.

Pain, which I strive to cure, were to be cruel.

ITHOCLES.

Nimble in vegeance, I forgive thee. Follow
Safety; with best success, O, may it prosper!—
Penthea, by thy side thy brother bleeds,　　　　　　　65
The earnest of his wrongs to thy forc'd faith.
Thoughts of ambition, or delicious banquet
With beauty, youth, and love, together perish
In my last breath, which on the sacred altar
Of a long-look'd-for peace—now—moves—to heaven.　　70

　　　　　　　　　　　　　　　　　　　　　　Moritur.

ORGILUS.

Farewell, fair spring of manhood; henceforth welcome
Best expectation of a noble suff'rance.
I'll lock the bodies safe, till what must follow
Shall be approv'd. —Sweet twins, shine stars forever.—
In vain they build their hopes whose life is shame;　　75
No monument lasts but a happy name.　　　　　*Exit* Orgilus.

[V.i]　　　　　　　　*Enter* Bassanes, *alone.*

BASSANES.

Athens, to Athens I have sent, the nursery
Of Greece for learning, and the fount of knowledge.
For here in Sparta there's not left amongst us
One wise man to direct; we're all turn'd madcaps.
'Tis said Apollo is the god of herbs;　　　　　　　5
Then certainly he knows the virtue of 'em.
To Delphos I have sent too; if there can be
A help for nature, we are sure yet.

　　　　　　　　　　Enter Orgilus.

ORGILUS.　　　　　　　　　　Honor

Attend thy counsels ever.

BASSANES.　　　　　　　　I beseech thee

7. too] *Weber;* to *Q.*

70.1. *Moritur*] He dies.
[V.i]
　5. *herbs*] Apollo was the god of healing as well as of music and poetry.

With all my heart, let me go from thee quietly;   10
I will not aught to do with thee of all men.
The doublers of a hare; or, in a morning,
Salutes from a splay-footed witch; to drop
Three drops of blood at th' nose just, and no more;
Croaking of ravens; or the screech of owls   15
Are not so boding mischief as thy crossing
My private meditations. Shun me, prithee;
And if I cannot love thee heartily,
I'll love thee as well as I can.

ORGILUS.   Noble Bassanes,
Mistake me not.

BASSANES.   Phew, then we shall be troubled.   20
Thou wert ordain'd my plague; heaven make me thankful.
And give me patience too, heaven, I beseech thee.

ORGILUS.
Accept a league of amity; for henceforth,
I vow by my best genius, in a syllable
Never to speak vexation. I will study   25
Service and friendship with a zealous sorrow
For my past incivility towards 'ee.

BASSANES.
Heyday, good words, good words! I must believe 'em,

11. aught] *Gifford;* ought *Q.*

---

12. *doublers*] "A hare is said to double, when she winds about in plain
fields to deceive the hounds" (Halliwell).

12. *hare*] "If an hare cross the high way, there are few above three-score
years that are not perplexed thereat" (Sir Thomas Browne's *Pseudodoxia
Epidemica*, V.22.i); proverbial, Tilley, H 150. According to Nares, "A *hare*
crossing a person's way was supposed to disorder his senses."

12–13. *in . . . witch*] Middleton refers to this superstition in *Women
Beware Women* (written *c.* 1621): "for of all creatures I cannot abide a splay-
footed woman. She's an unlucky thing to meet in a morning" (III.iii.111–
112).

13. *splay-footed*] having feet that are flat, spread out, and turned outward;
apparently a characteristic of witches: "Only her face and splayfoot have
made her accused for a witch" (Sidney's *Arcadia*, I, 21 [cf. II.ii.3–5, note]).

13–14. *to . . . more*] another unlucky omen, as indicated by Chapman in
All Fools (1605): "How now? my nose bleed? shall I write in blood? what,
only three drops? Sfoote this's ominous" (IV.i.343–345).

15. *Croaking . . . owls*] Browne, in *Pseudodoxia Epidemica*, describes ravens
and owls as "ominous appearers" (V.22.ii). Cf. Pliny X.xv, xvi.

24. *genius*] attendant spirit.

And be a coxcomb for my labor.

ORGILUS.   Use not

So hard a language; your misdoubt is causeless.   30

For instance, if you promise to put on

A constancy of patience—such a patience

As chronicle or history ne'er mentioned,

As follows not example but shall stand

A wonder and a theme for imitation,   35

The first, the index pointing to a second—

I will acquaint 'ee with an unmatch'd secret,

Whose knowledge to your griefs shall set a period.

BASSANES.

Thou canst not, Orgilus; 'tis in the power

Of the gods only. Yet for satisfaction,   40

Because I note an earnest in thine utterance,

Unforc'd and naturally free, be resolute.

The virgin bays shall not withstand the lightning

With a more careless danger than my constancy

The full of thy relation; could it move   45

Distraction in a senseless marble statue,

It should find me a rock. I do expect now

Some truth of unheard moment.

ORGILUS.   To your patience

You must add privacy, as strong in silence

As mysteries lock'd up in Jove's own bosom.   50

BASSANES.

A skull hid in the earth a treble age

Shall sooner prate.

ORGILUS.   Lastly, to such direction

As the severity of a glorious action

Deserves to lead your wisdom and your judgment,

You ought to yield obedience.

BASSANES.   With assurance   55

---

36. *index*] "that which serves to direct or point *to* a particular fact or conclusion; a guiding principle" (*OED*).

43–44. *bays . . . danger*] an allusion to the belief that the bay tree, or bay laurel, could not be harmed by lightning. Cf. Browne, *Pseudodoxia Epidemica*, II.vi.6 and Pliny XV.xl.

Of will and thankfulness.

ORGILUS.   With manly courage

Please then to follow me.

BASSANES.   Where'er, I fear not.   *Exeunt omnes.*

[V.ii]

Loud music. Enter Groneas *and* Hemophil, *leading* Euphranea; Christalla *and* Philema, *leading* Prophilus; Nearchus *supporting* Calantha; Crotolon *and* Amelus. *Cease loud music; all make a stand.*

CALANTHA.

We miss our servant Ithocles and Orgilus;
On whom attend they?

CROTOLON.   My son, gracious princess,

Whisper'd some new device, to which these revels
Should be but usher, wherein I conceive
Lord Ithocles and he himself are actors.   5

CALANTHA.

A fair excuse for absence. As for Bassanes,
Delights to him are troublesome. Armostes
Is with the king?

CROTOLON.   He is.

CALANTHA.   On to the dance.—

Dear cousin, hand you the bride; the bridegroom must be
Intrusted to my courtship. —Be not jealous,   10
Euphranea; I shall scarcely prove a temptress.—
Fall to our dance.

Music.

Nearchus *dance with* Euphranea, Prophilus *with* Calantha, Christalla *with* Hemophil, Philema *with* Groneas. *Dance the first change, during which enter* Armostes.

ARMOSTES (*in* Calantha's *ear*).   The king your father's dead.

9. hand you the bride] *Q (corr.)*;
hand you with the bride *Q (uncorr.).*

___

9. *hand*] lead or conduct by the hand.
12–27. *Fall .... bluntly*] This incident may have been suggested to Ford by Marston's *The Malcontent* (1604), in which Altofront (Malevole) and Pietro reveal themselves to their wives between measures of a dance (V.vi).
12.3. *change*] a round in dancing.

CALANTHA.

To the other change.

ARMOSTES.   Is't possible?

Dance again. Enter Bassanes.

BASSANES (*in* Calantha's *ear*).   O, madam,
Penthea, poor Penthea's starv'd!

CALANTHA.   Beshrew thee.—
Lead to the next.

BASSANES.   Amazement dulls my senses.   15

Dance again. Enter Orgilus.

ORGILUS (*in* Calantha's *ear*).
Brave Ithocles is murder'd, murder'd cruelly.

CALANTHA.

How dull this music sounds! Strike up more sprightly;
Our footings are not active like our heart,
Which treads the nimbler measure.

ORGILUS.   I am thunderstruck.

Last change. Cease music.

CALANTHA.

So, let us breathe awhile. Hath not this motion   20
Rais'd fresher color on your cheeks?

NEARCHUS.   Sweet princess,
A perfect purity of blood enamels
The beauty of your white.

CALANTHA.   We all look cheerfully.
And cousin, 'tis, methinks, a rare presumption
In any who prefers our lawful pleasures   25
Before their own sour censure, to interrupt
The custom of this ceremony bluntly.

NEARCHUS.

None dares, lady.

CALANTHA.

Yes, yes; some hollow voice deliver'd to me

---

18. *footings*] "moving with measured tread, dancing" (*OED*).
19. *measure*] "a grave solemn dance, with slow and measured steps, like
the minuet . . . . the phrase was *to tread a measure*" (Nares).

How that the king was dead.

ARMOSTES.   The king is dead.   30

That fatal news was mine; for in mine arms

He breath'd his last, and with his crown bequeath'd 'ee

Your mother's wedding ring, which here I tender.

CROTOLON.

Most strange!

CALANTHA.   Peace crown his ashes. We are queen, then.

NEARCHUS.

Long live Calantha, Sparta's sovereign queen!   35

OMNES.

Long live the queen!

CALANTHA.   What whispered Bassanes?

BASSANES.

That my Penthea, miserable soul,

Was starv'd to death.

CALANTHA.   She's happy; she hath finish'd

A long and painful progress. —A third murmur

Pierc'd mine unwilling ears.

ORGILUS.   That Ithocles   40

Was murder'd; rather butcher'd, had not bravery

Of an undaunted spirit, conquering terror,

Proclaim'd his last act triumph over ruin.

ARMOSTES.

How? Murder'd!

CALANTHA.   By whose hand?

ORGILUS.   By mine; this weapon

Was instrument to my revenge. The reasons   45

Are just and known; quit him of these, and then

Never liv'd gentleman of greater merit,

Hope, or abiliment to steer a kingdom.

CROTOLON.

Fie, Orgilus!

EUPHRANEA.   Fie, brother!

CALANTHA.   You have done it?

BASSANES.

How it was done let him report, the forfeit   50

---

46. *quit*] acquit.
48. *abiliment*] "capacity, qualification" (Spencer).

Of whose allegiance to our laws doth covet
Rigor of justice; but that done it is,
Mine eyes have been an evidence of credit
Too sure to be convinc'd. —Armostes, rent not
Thine arteries with hearing the bare circumstances   55
Of these calmities. Thou'st lost a nephew,
A niece, and I a wife. Continue man still;
Make me the pattern of digesting evils,
Who can outlive my mighty ones, not shrinking
At such a pressure as would sink a soul   60
Into what's most of death, the worst of horrors.
But I have seal'd a covenant with sadness,
And enter'd into bonds without condition,
To stand these tempests calmly. —Mark me, nobles,
I do not shed a tear, not for Penthea.   65
Excellent misery!

CALANTHA.   We begin our reign
With a first act of justice. —Thy confession,
Unhappy Orgilus, dooms thee a sentence.
But yet thy father's or thy sister's presence
Shall be excus'd. —Give, Crotolon, a blessing   70
To thy lost son. —Euphranea, take a farewell,
And both be gone.

CROTOLON.   Confirm thee, noble sorrow,
In worthy resolution.

EUPHRANEA.   Could my tears speak,
My griefs were slight.

ORGILUS.   All goodness dwell amongst ye.—
Enjoy my sister, Prophilus; my vengeance   75
Aim'd never at thy prejudice.

CALANTHA.   Now withdraw.—

                Exeunt Crotolon, Prophilus, *et* Euphranea.
Bloody relater of thy stains in blood
(For that thou hast reported him whose fortunes
And life by thee are both at once snatch'd from him,

73. Could] *Q (corr.);* Cculd *Q*   74. goodness] *Weber;* gooddesse *Q.*
(uncorr.).

---

54. *convinc'd*] confuted.   54. *rent*] rend.
76. *prejudice*] harm.

With honorable mention), make thy choice   80
Of what death likes thee best; there's all our bounty.—
But to excuse delays, let me, dear cousin,
Entreat you and these lords see execution
Instant before 'ee part.

NEARCHUS.   Your will commands us.

ORGILUS.

One suit, just queen, my last; vouchsafe your clemency   85
That by no common hand I be divided
From this my humble frailty.

CALANTHA.   To their wisdoms
Who are to be spectators of thine end,
I make the reference. Those that are dead
Are dead; had they not now died, of necessity   90
They must have paid the debt they ow'd to nature,
One time or other. —Use dispatch, my lords;
We'll suddenly prepare our coronation.

                            Exeunt Calantha, Philema, Christalla.

ARMOSTES.

'Tis strange these tragedies should never touch on
Her female pity.

BASSANES.   She has a masculine spirit.   95
And wherefore should I pule, and like a girl
Put finger in the eye? Let's be all toughness,
Without distinction betwixt sex and sex.

NEARCHUS.

Now Orgilus, thy choice?

ORGILUS.   To bleed to death.

ARMOSTES.

The executioner?

ORGILUS.   Myself, no surgeon.   100
I am well skill'd in letting blood. Bind fast

---

81. *likes*] pleases.

87. *humble frailty*] i.e., existence, life.

96. *pule*] cry in a thin or weak voice, whine.

99. *To . . . death*] The famous Stoic Seneca, sentenced to death by Nero, killed himself in this manner (Tacitus, *Annals*, XV, 60–64).

101–103. *Bind . . . stream*] "In performing the operation of bleeding, formerly so common, the arm was bound above the spot selected in order to distend the veins. For the same reason the patient grasped a staff" (Ellis).

This arm, that so the pipes may from their conduits
Convey a full stream. Here's a skillful instrument.

                            [Shows his dagger.]

Only I am a beggar to some charity
To speed me in this execution,   105
By lending th'other prick to th'tother arm
When this is bubbling life out.

BASSANES.   I am for 'ee.
It most concerns my art, my care, my credit.—
Quick, fillet both his arms.

ORGILUS.   Gramercy, friendship.
Such courtesies are real which flow cheerfully   110
Without an expectation of requital.
Reach me a staff in this hand. If a proneness
Or custom in my nature, from my cradle,
Had been inclin'd to fierce and eager bloodshed,
A coward guilt, hid in a coward quaking,   115
Would have betray'd fame to ignoble flight
And vagabond pursuit of dreadful safety.
But look upon my steadiness, and scorn not
The sickness of my fortune, which since Bassanes
Was husband to Penthea had lain bedrid.   120
We trifle time in words. Thus I show cunning
In opening of a vein too full, too lively.   *[Opens a vein.]*

ARMOSTES.
Desperate courage!

NEARCHUS.   Honorable infamy!

HEMOPHIL.
I tremble at the sight.

GRONEAS.   Would I were loose!

---

109. his] *Weber;* this *Q.*   123. S.P. NEARCHUS] *Gifford; speech
assigned to* Orgilus *in Q.*

---

104. *beggar . . . charity*] i.e., dependent upon some kindness.
109. *fillet*] "bind with a narrow strip, to facilitate the blood-letting"
(Spencer). In some plays realism was achieved by means of a blood-
saturated sponge held in the actor's palm and pressed against his "wounded"
face or limb, but this device would not do for the "bleeding" of Orgilus,
since his "arms were bared, tape was tied round his elbows, and he held sticks
in his hands" (Lawrence).
116. *fame*] reputation.

BASSANES.

    It sparkles like a lusty wine new broach'd;   125
    The vessel must be sound from which it issues.—
    Grasp hard this other stick; I'll be as nimble.
    But prithee look not pale. Have at 'ee; stretch out
    Thine arm with vigor and unshook virtue.   [*Opens another vein.*]
    Good! O, I envy not a rival fitted   130
    To conquer in extremities. This pastime
    Appears majestical; some high-tun'd poem
    Hereafter shall deliver to posterity
    The writer's glory and his subject's triumph.
    How is 't, man? Droop not yet.

ORGILUS.   I feel no palsies.   135

    On a pair-royal do I wait in death:
    My sovereign, as his liegeman; on my mistress,
    As a devoted servant; and on Ithocles,
    As if no brave yet no unworthy enemy.
    Nor did I use an engine to entrap   140
    His life, out of a slavish fear to combat
    Youth, strength, or cunning, but for that I durst not
    Engage the goodness of a cause on fortune,
    By which his name might have outfac'd my vengeance.
    Ah Tecnicus, inspir'd with Phoebus' fire,   145
    I call to mind thy augury; 'twas perfect:
    Revenge proves its own executioner.
    When feeble man is bending to his mother,
    The dust 'a was first fram'd on, thus he totters.

BASSANES.

    Life's fountain is dried up.

ORGILUS.   So falls the standards   150

    Of my prerogative in being a creature.

---

145. Ah] *Yale Q (first letter unreadable*   *Weber and all subsequent editors.*
in six other copies examined); Oh

---

    125. *broach'd*] tapped.
    136. *pair-royal*] in card games, three cards of the same denomination, as three sixes or three kings; here also an allusion to the personages being described.
    142. *cunning*] skill.   143. *Engage*] stake.
    150. *standards*] flags, ensigns.
    151. *prerogative*] natural advantage or privilege.

A mist hangs o'er mine eyes; the sun's bright splendor
Is clouded in an everlasting shadow.
Welcome, thou ice that sitt'st about my heart;
No heat can ever thaw thee.   *Dies.*

NEARCHUS.   Speech hath left him.   155

BASSANES.

'A has shook hands with time. His funeral urn
Shall be my charge. Remove the bloodless body.
The coronation must require attendance;
That past, my few days can be but one mourning.   *Exeunt.*

[V.iii]

An altar covered with white, two lights of virgin wax; during which music of
recorders. Enter four bearing Ithocles on a hearse, or in a chair, in a rich robe,
and a crown on his head; place him on one side of the altar. After him enter
Calantha *in a white robe and crown'd;* Euphranea, Philema, Christalla,
in white; Nearchus, Armostes, Crotolon, Prophilus, Amelus, Bassanes,
Hemophil, *and* Groneas. Calantha *goes and kneels before the altar; the*
rest stand off, the women kneeling behind. Cease recorders during her devotions.
Soft music. Calantha *and the rest rise, doing obeisance to the altar.*

CALANTHA.

Our orisons are heard; the gods are merciful.
Now tell me, you whose loyalties pays tribute
To us your lawful sovereign, how unskillful
Your duties or obedience is, to render
Subjection to the scepter of a virgin,   5
Who have been ever fortunate in princes
Of masculine and stirring composition.
A woman has enough to govern wisely
Her own demeanors, passions, and divisions.
A nation warlike and inur'd to practice   10
Of policy and labor cannot brook
A feminate authority. We therefore
Command your counsel how you may advise us
In choosing of a husband whose abilities
Can better guide this kingdom.

0.2. *recorders*] "a wind instrument of the flute or flageolet kind" (*OED*).
1. *orisons*] prayers.   9. *divisions*] discords.

NEARCHUS.   Royal lady,   15
    Your law is in your will.
ARMOSTES.   We have seen tokens
    Of constancy too lately to mistrust it.
CROTOLON.
    Yet if your highness settle on a choice
    By your own judgment both allow'd and lik'd of,
    Sparta may grow in power and proceed   20
    To an increasing height.
CALANTHA [to Bassanes].   Hold you the same mind?
BASSANES.
    Alas, great mistress, reason is so clouded
    With the thick darkness of my infinite woes
    That I forecast nor dangers, hopes, or safety.
    Give me some corner of the world to wear out   25
    The remnant of the minutes I must number,
    Where I may hear no sounds but sad complaints
    Of virgins who have lost contracted partners,
    Of husbands howling that their wives were ravish'd
    By some untimely fate, of friends divided   30
    By churlish opposition, or of fathers
    Weeping upon their children's slaughtered carcasses,
    Or daughters groaning o'er their father's hearses,
    And I can dwell there, and with these keep consort
    As musical as theirs. What can you look for   35
    From an old, foolish, peevish, doting man
    But craziness of age?
CALANTHA.
    Cousin of Argos.
NEARCHUS.   Madam?
CALANTHA.   Were I presently
    To choose you for my lord, I'll open freely
    What articles I would propose to treat on   40
    Before our marriage.
NEARCHUS.   Name them, virtuous lady.
CALANTHA.
    I would presume you would retain the royalty

23. infinite] *Weber;* infinites *Q.*

---

34. *consort*] harmony.

Of Sparta in her own bounds. Then in Argos
Armostes might be viceroy; in Messene
Might Crotolon bear sway; and Bassanes— 45

BASSANES.

I, queen? Alas, what I?

CALANTHA.   Be Sparta's marshall.
The multitudes of high employments could not
But set a peace to private griefs. —[*To* Nearchus.]   These
                                                 gentlemen,
Groneas and Hemophil, with worthy pensions,
Should wait upon your person in your chamber.   50
I would bestow Christalla on Amelus;
She'll prove a constant wife. And Philema
Should into Vesta's temple.

BASSANES.   This is a testament;
It sounds not like conditions on a marriage.

NEARCHUS.

All this should be perform'd.

CALANTHA.   Lastly, for Prophilus,   55
He should be, cousin, solemnly invested
In all those honors, titles, and preferments
Which his dear friend and my neglected husband
Too short a time enjoy'd.

PROPHILUS.   I am unworthy
To live in your remembrance.

EUPHRANEA.   Excellent lady!   60

NEARCHUS.

Madam, what means that word "neglected husband"?

CALANTHA.

Forgive me. —Now I turn to thee, thou shadow
Of my contracted lord. —Bear witness all,
I put my mother's wedding ring upon
His finger; 'twas my father's last bequest.   65
Thus I new marry him whose wife I am;
Death shall not separate us. O, my lords,
I but deceiv'd your eyes with antic gesture,
When one news straight came huddling on another

64. mother's] *Weber;* mother *Q.*

---

68. *antic*] "absurd from fantastic incongruity; grotesque" (*OED*).

Of death, and death, and death. Still I danc'd forward;   70
But it struck home, and here, and in an instant.
Be such mere women, who with shrieks and outcries
Can vow a present end to all their sorrows,
Yet live to vow new pleasures, and outlive them.
They are the silent griefs which cut the heartstrings;   75
Let me die smiling.

NEARCHUS.   'Tis a truth too ominous.

CALANTHA.

One kiss on these cold lips, my last—   [*Kisses* Ithocles.]
                    crack, crack!—
Argos now's Sparta's king. —Command the voices
Which wait at th'altar, now to sing the song
I fitted for my end.

NEARCHUS.   Sirs, the song.   80

A Song.

ALL.   *Glories, pleasures, pomps, delights, and ease*
                    Can but please
              Th'outward senses when the mind
              Is not untroubled or by peace refin'd.

1 [VOICE].   *Crowns may flourish and decay;*   85
              Beauties shine, but fade away.

2 [VOICE].   *Youth may revel, yet it must*
              Lie down in a bed of dust.

3 [VOICE].   *Earthly honors flow and waste;*
              Time alone doth change and last.   90

ALL.   *Sorrows mingled with contents prepare*
                    Rest for care;
              Love only reigns in death, though art
              Can find no comfort for a broken heart.   [Calantha *dies.*]

ARMOSTES.

Look to the queen!

83. *Th'outward*] *Gifford; outward Q.*

---

80. *fitted*] prepared, made ready.
84. *not*] "Gifford says 'I can only reduce it to some tolerable meaning by
reading *or* before *untroubled* instead of *not*.' But if one properly emphasizes
outward the sense of the quarto is sufficiently clear, in spite of the slight
obscurity of the double negative: glories . . . can please only the *outward*
enses when the mind is troubled or not refined by peace" (Sherman).

BASSANES.   Her heart is broke indeed.
O, royal maid, would thou hadst miss'd this part;
Yet 'twas a brave one. I must weep to see
Her smile in death.

ARMOSTES.   Wise Tecnicus! Thus said he:
When youth is ripe and age from time doth part,
The lifeless trunk shall wed the broken heart.   100
'Tis here fulfill'd.

NEARCHUS.   I am your king.

OMNES.   Long live
Nearchus, King of Sparta!

NEARCHUS.   Her last will
Shall never be digress'd from; wait in order
Upon these faithful lovers as becomes us.—
The counsels of the gods are never known   105
Till men can call th'effects of them their own.   [*Exeunt.*]

FINIS

The Epilogue

Where noble judgments and clear eyes are fix'd
To grace endeavor, there sits truth not mix'd
With ignorance. Those censures may command
Belief which talk not till they understand.
Let some say, "This was flat"; some, "Here the scene   5
Fell from its height"; another, that the mean
Was "ill observ'd" in such a growing passion
As it transcended either state or fashion.
Some few may cry, "'Twas pretty well" or "So,
But—" and there shrug in silence. Yet we know   10
Our writer's aim was in the whole address'd
Well to deserve of *all*, but please the *best*;
Which granted, by th'allowance of this strain,
The *Broken Heart* may be piec'd up again.

FINIS

7. Was] *Weber;* W *followed by one*
or two illegible lower-case letters in Q.

6. *the mean*] proper moderation.

Appendix

Chronology

Approximate years are indicated by *, occurrences in doubt by (?).

Political and Literary Events	*Life and Major Works of John Ford*

1558
Accession of Queen Elizabeth I.
Robert Greene born.
Thomas Kyd born.

1560
George Chapman born.

1561
Francis Bacon born.

1564
Shakespeare born.
Christopher Marlowe born.

1572
Thomas Dekker born.*
John Donne born.
Massacre of St. Bartholomew's Day.

1573
Ben Jonson born.*

1574
Thomas Heywood born.*

1576
The Theatre, the first permanent public theater in London, established by James Burbage.
John Marston born.

1577
The Curtain theater opened.
Holinshed's *Chronicles of England, Scotland and Ireland.*

Drake begins circumnavigation of
the earth; completed 1580.

1578
John Lyly's *Euphues: The Anatomy of
Wit.*

1579
John Fletcher born.
Sir Thomas North's translation of
Plutarch's *Lives.*

1580
Thomas Middleton born.

1583
Philip Massinger born.

1584
Francis Beaumont born.*

1586
Death of Sir Philip Sidney.

John Ford born at Islington,
Devonshire, April 17.

1587
The Rose theater opened by
Henslowe.
Marlowe's *TAMBURLAINE*, Part
I.*
Execution of Mary, Queen of Scots.
Drake raids Cadiz.

1588
Defeat of the Spanish Armada.
Marlowe's *TAMBURLAINE*, Part
II.*

1589
Greene's *FRIAR BACON AND
FRIAR BUNGAY.*
Marlowe's *THE JEW OF
MALTA.*
Kyd's *THE SPANISH TRAGEDY.*

1590
Spenser's *Faerie Queene* (Books I–III)
published.
Sidney's *Arcadia* published.
Shakespeare's *HENRY VI*, Parts
I–III,* *TITUS ANDRONICUS.*

1591

Shakespeare's *RICHARD III.**

1592

Marlowe's *DOCTOR FAUSTUS** and *EDWARD II.**
Shakespeare's *TAMING OF THE SHREW** and *THE COMEDY OF ERRORS.**
Death of Greene.

1593

Shakespeare's *LOVE'S LABOR'S LOST*;* *Venus and Adonis* published.
Death of Marlowe.
Theaters closed on account of plague.

1594

Shakespeare's *TWO GENTLE-MEN OF VERONA*;* *The Rape of Lucrece* published.
Shakespeare's company becomes Lord Chamberlain's Men.
Death of Kyd.

1595

The Swan theater built.
Sidney's *Defense of Poesy* published.
Shakespeare's *ROMEO AND JULIET,** *A MIDSUMMER NIGHT'S DREAM,** *RICHARD II.**
Raleigh's first expedition to Guiana.

1596

Spenser's *Faerie Queene* (Books IV–VI) published.
Shakespeare's *MERCHANT OF VENICE,** *KING JOHN.**
James Shirley born.

1597

Bacon's *Essays* (first edition).
Shakespeare's *HENRY IV*, Part I.*

1598

Demolition of The Theatre.
Shakespeare's *MUCH ADO*

ABOUT NOTHING, HENRY IV,
Part II.*
Jonson's *EVERY MAN IN HIS
HUMOR* (first version).
Seven books of Chapman's trans-
lation of Homer's *Iliad* published.

1599
The Paul's Boys reopen their
theater.
The Globe theater opened.
Shakespeare's *AS YOU LIKE IT,*
HENRY V, JULIUS CAESAR.*
Marston's *ANTONIO AND MEL-
LIDA,* Parts I and II.
Dekker's *THE SHOEMAKERS'
HOLIDAY.*
Death of Spenser.

1600
Shakespeare's *TWELFTH
NIGHT.*
The Fortune theater built by Alleyn.
The Children of the Chapel begin
to play at the Blackfriars.

1601
Shakespeare's *HAMLET,* MERRY
WIVES OF WINDSOR.*   Brief residence at Oxford (?).
Insurrection and execution of the
Earl of Essex.
Jonson's *POETASTER.*

1602
Shakespeare's *TROILUS AND*   Admitted to the Middle Temple,
CRESSIDA.   November 16.

1603
Death of Queen Elizabeth I;
accession of James VI of Scotland
as James I.
Florio's translation of Montaigne's
Essays published.
Shakespeare's *ALL'S WELL THAT
ENDS WELL.*
Heywood's *A WOMAN KILLED
WITH KINDNESS.*

Marston's *THE MALCONTENT.**
Shakespeare's company becomes the
King's Men.

1604
Shakespeare's *MEASURE FOR
MEASURE,* OTHELLO.**
Marston's *THE FAWN.**
Chapman's *BUSSY D'AMBOIS.**

1605
Shakespeare's *KING LEAR.**
Marston's *THE DUTCH COUR-
TESAN.**
Bacon's *Advancement of Learning*
published.
The Gunpowder Plot.

Expelled from the Middle Temple
for not paying buttery bill.

1606
Shakespeare's *MACBETH.**
Jonson's *VOLPONE.**
Tourneur's *REVENGER'S
TRAGEDY.**
The Red Bull theater built.
Death of John Lyly.

Publication of *Fame's Memorial*
(poem) and *Honor Triumphant* (pamphlet).
Barnes's *Four Books of Offices*, with
commendatory verses by Ford, and
Cooper's *Funeral Tears for the Death
of the Earl of Devonshire*, with a poem
by Ford, published.

1607
Shakespeare's *ANTONY AND
CLEOPATRA.**
Beaumont's *KNIGHT OF THE
BURNING PESTLE.**
Settlement of Jamestown, Virginia.

1608
Shakespeare's *CORIOLANUS,*
TIMON OF ATHENS,*
PERICLES.**
Chapman's *CONSPIRACY AND
TRAGEDY OF CHARLES, DUKE
OF BYRON.**
Dekker's *Gull's Hornbook* published.
Richard Burbage leases Blackfriars
theater for King's company.
John Milton born.

Reinstated at the Middle Temple,
June 10.

1609

Shakespeare's *CYMBELINE*;* *Sonnets* published.

Jonson's *EPICOENE*.

1610

Jonson's *ALCHEMIST*.

Chapman's *REVENGE OF BUSSY D'AMBOIS.**

Richard Crashaw born.

1611

Authorized (King James) version of the Bible published.

Shakespeare's *THE WINTER'S TALE,* *THE TEMPEST.**

Beaumont and Fletcher's *A KING AND NO KING*.

Tourneur's *ATHEIST'S TRAGEDY.**

Middleton's *A CHASTE MAID IN CHEAPSIDE.**

Chapman's translation of *Iliad* completed.

1612

Webster's *THE WHITE DEVIL.**

1613

The Globe theater burned.

Shakespeare's *HENRY VIII* (with Fletcher).

Webster's *THE DUCHESS OF MALFI.**

Sir Thomas Overbury murdered.

1614

The Globe theater rebuilt.

The Hope theater built.

Jonson's *BARTHOLOMEW FAIR*.

1615

1616

Publication of Folio edition of Jonson's *WORKS*.

Chapman's *Whole Works of Homer*.

Receives total bequest of £10 upon the death of his father, Thomas Ford.

Christ's Bloody Sweat (poem) and *The Golden Mean* (pamphlet) published.

Sir Thomas Overbury's Ghost (book; not extant) entered in the Stationers' Register, November 25.

Granted £20 per year by will of his older brother, Henry, September 17.

Death of Shakespeare.
Death of Beaumont.
1617

One of forty members of the Middle Temple admonished for wearing hats instead of lawyers' caps.

1618
Outbreak of Thirty Years War.
Execution of Raleigh.
1620
Settlement of Plymouth, Massachusetts.

A Line of Life (pamphlet) published.

1621
Middleton's *WOMEN BEWARE WOMEN.**
Robert Burton's *Anatomy of Melancholy* published.
Andrew Marvell born.

THE WITCH OF EDMONTON, with Dekker and Rowley.

1622
Middleton and Rowley's *THE CHANGELING.**
Henry Vaughan born.
1623
Publication of Folio edition of Shakespeare's *COMEDIES, HISTORIES, AND TRAGEDIES.*

THE SPANISH GYPSY (?), with Middleton and Rowley (Lady Elizabeth's company).
Webster's *THE DUCHESS OF MALFI* and Cockeram's *The English Dictionary*, both with commendatory verses by Ford, published.

1624

THE SUN'S DARLING, with Dekker, licensed by Herbert.
THE BRISTOW MERCHANT (lost) and *THE FAIRY KNIGHT* (lost [?]), both with Dekker.
THE LATE MURDER OF THE SON UPON THE MOTHER (lost), with Dekker, Rowley, and Webster.

1625
Death of King James I; accession of Charles I.
Death of Fletcher.

THE FAIR MAID OF THE INN, with Fletcher, Massinger, and Webster.

1626
Death of Tourneur.
Death of Bacon.
1627
Death of Middleton.
1628
Petition of Right.   *THE LOVER'S MELANCHOLY*
Buckingham assassinated.   (published 1629).
1629

Shirley's *THE WEDDING* and
Massinger's *THE ROMAN ACTOR*,
both with commendatory verses by
Ford, published.

1630

*BEAUTY IN A TRANCE** (lost).

1631
Shirley's *THE TRAITOR*.
Death of Donne.
John Dryden born.
1632
Massinger's *THE CITY MADAM*.*   Brome's *THE NORTHERN LASS*,
with commendatory verses by Ford,
published.

1633
Donne's *Poems* published.   *THE BROKEN HEART, LOVE'S
Death of George Herbert.   SACRIFICE*, and *'TIS PITY SHE'S
A WHORE* published.

1634
Death of Chapman, Marston,   *PERKIN WARBECK* published.
Webster.*
Publication of *THE TWO NOBLE
KINSMEN*, with title-page attri-
bution to Shakespeare and Fletcher.
Milton's *Comus*.

1635
Sir Thomas Browne's *Religio Medici*.
1636

Massinger's *THE GREAT DUKE
OF FLORENCE*, with commendatory verses by Ford, published.

1637
Death of Jonson.

1638

THE LADY'S TRIAL licensed.
THE FANCIES CHASTE AND NOBLE published.
Jonsonus Virbius, with commendatory verses by Ford, published.

1639
First Bishops' War.
Death of Carew.*

Publication of *THE LADY'S TRIAL*, with dedication signed by Ford.
No certain later record of Ford.

1640
Short Parliament.
Long Parliament impeaches Laud.
Death of Massinger, Burton.

1641
Irish rebel.
Death of Heywood.

1642
Charles I leaves London; Civil War breaks out.
Shirley's *COURT SECRET*.
All theaters closed by Act of Parliament.

1643
Parliament swears to the Solemn League and Covenant.

1645
Ordinance for New Model Army enacted.

1646
End of First Civil War.

1647
Army occupies London.
Charles I forms alliance with Scots.
Publication of Folio edition of Beaumont and Fletcher's *COMEDIES AND TRAGEDIES*.

1648
Second Civil War.

1649
Execution of Charles I.

1650

Jeremy Collier born.

1651

Hobbes' *Leviathan* published.

1652

First Dutch War began (ended 1654).

Thomas Otway born.

1653

Nathaniel Lee born.*

THE QUEEN published.

1656

D'Avenant's *THE SIEGE OF RHODES* performed at Rutland House.

1657

John Dennis born.

1658

Death of Oliver Cromwell.

D'Avenant's *THE CRUELTY OF THE SPANIARDS IN PERU* performed at the Cockpit.

Howard's *THE GREAT FAVOR- ITE, OR THE DUKE OF LERMA*, possibly a rewriting of some earlier play by Ford, published.

1660

Restoration of Charles II.

Theatrical patents granted to Thomas Killigrew and Sir William D'Avenant, authorizing them to form, respectively, the King's and the Duke of York's Companies.

AN ILL BEGINNING HAS A GOOD END (lost), *THE LONDON MERCHANT* (lost), and *THE ROYAL COMBAT* (lost) all entered in the Stationers' Register and attributed to Ford by Moseley.

1661

Cowley's *THE CUTTER OF COLEMAN STREET*.

D'Avenant's *THE SIEGE OF RHODES* (expanded to two parts).

1662

Charter granted to the Royal Society.

1663

Dryden's *THE WILD GALLANT*.

Tuke's *THE ADVENTURES OF FIVE HOURS*.

1664

Sir John Vanbrugh born.

Dryden's *THE RIVAL LADIES.*
Dryden and Howard's *THE INDIAN QUEEN.*
Etherege's *THE COMICAL REVENGE.*

1665
Second Dutch War began (ended 1667).
Great Plague.
Dryden's *THE INDIAN EMPEROR.*
Orrery's *MUSTAPHA.*

1666
Fire of London.
Death of James Shirley.